More Excel
OUTSIDE
THE BOX

by
Bob Umlas

Holy Macro! Books
PO Box 82
Uniontown OH 44685

More Excel Outside the Box

Printed in the USA by Hess Print Solutions

First Printing: May 2015

Author: Bob Umlas

Cover Design: Shannon Mattiza 6Ft4 Productions

Publisher: Bill Jelen

Index: Nellie Jay

Proofreader: Kurt Nichols

Published by Holy Macro! Books, PO Box 82, Uniontown OH 44685

Distributed by Independent Publishers Group, Chicago IL

ISBN 978-1-615470-036-5

Library of Congress Control Number: 2015940631

Table of Contents

Other books by Bob Umlas:
This isn't Excel, it's Magic (2005)
This isn't Excel, it's Magic 2nd Edition (2007)
Excel Outside the Box (2012)

Introduction

There are many Excel books out there; why did I write this one? My daily work involves writing custom applications using Excel and there are many problems I've had to think through to come up with a solution in Excel. My previous book, Excel Outside the Box, tackled many of these problems, and I came up against several more – enough to write another book!

I've used these solutions many times in my applications. I have not found any books or articles which described similar issues and solutions, yet it is hard to imagine that Excel developers in other companies hadn't also come up against these issues. So, given the feedback from my previous version of this book, I thought it was time for another book to help the already-advanced Excel developer get past these hurdles.

User Interface Topics

This section explores many ways to validate data, rearrange data, change how data appears, etc. in ways likely not seen before. It explores Conditional Formatting, formulas, some VBA, and more techniques which you will find interesting.

Using a Conditional Formatting On/Off Switch

This worksheet uses conditional formatting to highlight each cell that contains a value over 50:

A1				f_x	=RAND()*100

	A	B	C	D	E	F
1	43.22501	11.18166	25.7966	9.397823	57.65467	
2	33.5903	39.47272	8.916447	34.5876	81.66759	
3	0.202516	95.82382	70.07503	89.95508	11.98697	
4	93.99169	89.37614	9.964088	2.805748	94.64908	

There are several ways to get this kind of conditional formatting. One way is to use Highlight Cells Rules, as shown here:

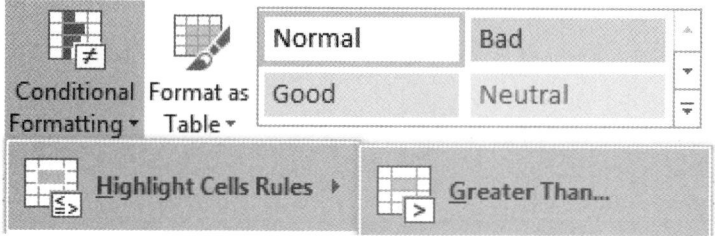

The worksheet above uses a formula, like this:

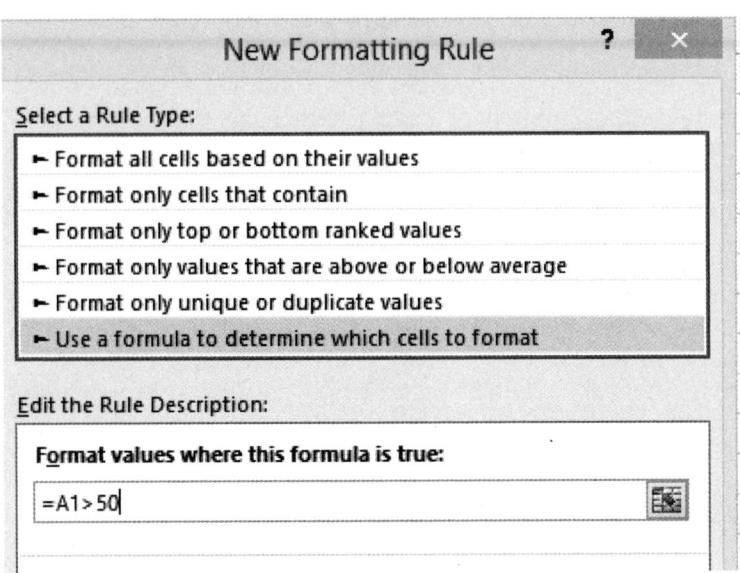

This type of conditional formatting can be really helpful, but you might want to be able to turn it on and off in a worksheet. In that case, you could put a data validation switch in cell I1, like this:

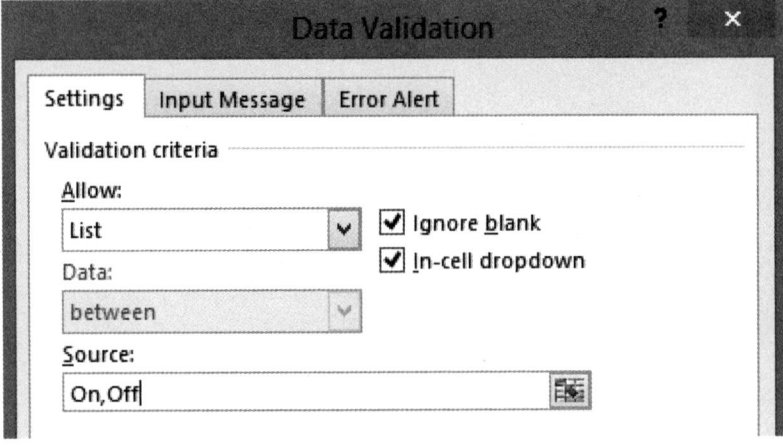

Then you could change the formula to this:

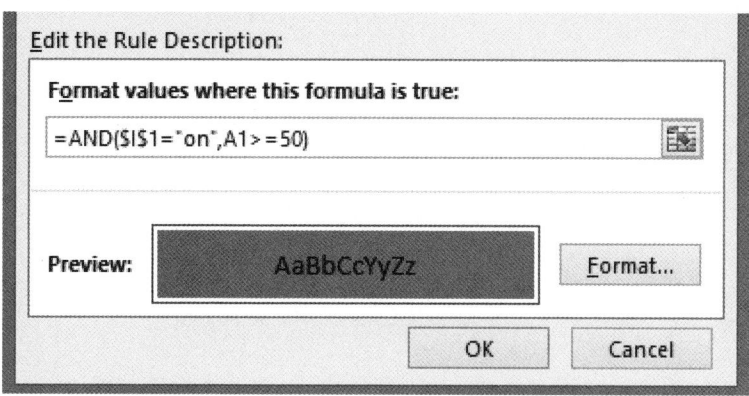

Your worksheet would then look like this with the conditional formatting turned on:

	A	B	C	D	E	F	G	H	I
1	75.53261	28.50663	22.70841	69.90838	77.54031				On
2	23.58725	6.884626	91.43047	70.92872	82.54125				
3	97.45856	11.12011	47.62344	50.68533	17.81584				
4	61.93464	63.17354	9.330976	16.69923	9.05546				

And it would look like this with the conditional formatting turned off:

	A	B	C	D	E	F	G	H	I
1	30.3854	49.09215	46.95324	63.13005	13.19592				Off
2	27.46848	32.39832	91.83917	68.68445	91.9697				
3	92.67428	42.86056	50.01013	35.47103	21.97394				
4	32.65817	81.27511	72.95503	44.82539	62.2963				
5	4.507351	79.82249	83.62686	52.78902	28.1525				
6	94.022	57.16752	80.94169	35.70417	6.819062				
7	72.32463	66.40099	73.46495	56.10181	27.21584				
8	2.422646	46.58629	72.70834	81.90069	26.07642				
9	68.40136	73.47959	58.8948	11.54196	39.94174				
10	61.74265	33.30622	26.91939	12.47001	56.02141				
11	37.47752	50.02521	32.15704	4.805255	15.02422				
12	1.995138	33.01791	37.76152	95.55732	25.34802				

(The numbers keep changing here because the RAND function is used in the formulas in all the cells.)

Using Data Validation to Prohibit Entry of Digits

This figure shows an invalid entry error:

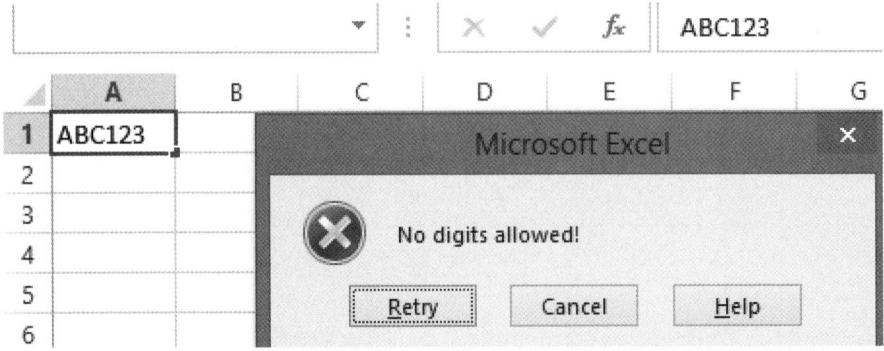

This isn't a valid entry because there are digits in cell A1, and the worksheet is set up to allow only letters. To avoid getting this type of error, you can use data validation.

A data validation formula is a custom formula that appears in the Data Validation dialog:

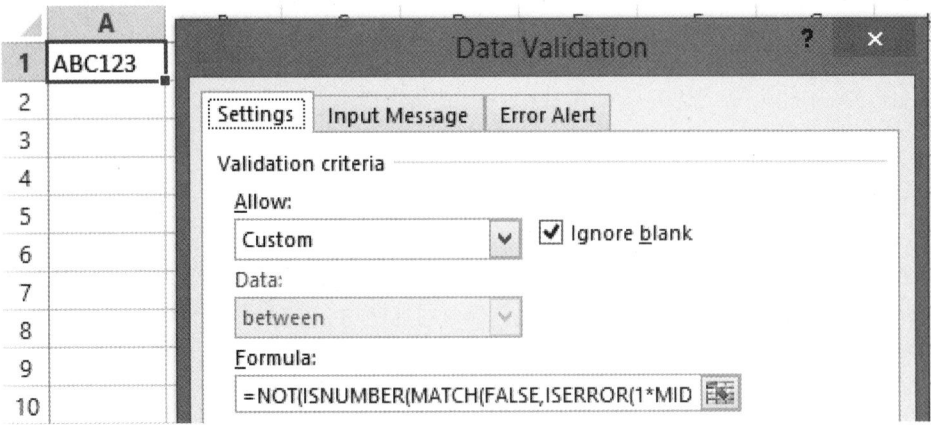

Here's the complete formula:

=NOT(ISNUMBER(MATCH(FALSE,ISERROR(1*MID(A1,ROW(INDI-RECT("1:"&LEN(A1))),1)),0)))

Normally, as a worksheet function, this would need to be entered as an array (using Ctrl+Shift+Enter), but you can't enter a formula that way in the Data Validation dialog. Therefore, Excel treats any formula you enter as if it were an array formula.

This formula examines each character in cell A1 and multiplies it by 1 to determine whether it's a number. If it is a number, then it shouldn't be allowed.

Let's examine how this works with the ABC123 entry from the inside out (using F9 for each step):

IRECT("1:"&LEN(A1)),1)),(becomes NDIRECT("1:6")),1)),

.ROW(INDIRECT("1:6")) becomes MID(A1,{1;2;3;4;5;6},1)).

MID(A1,{1;2;3;4;5;6},1)) becomes {"A";"B";"C";"1";"2";"3"}),

(1*{"A";"B";"C";"1";"2";"3"}) becomes {#VALUE!;#VALUE!;#VALUE!;1;2;3}) (note the 1;2;3 at the end).

ISERROR({#VALUE!;#VALUE!;#VALUE!;1;2;3}) becomes {TRUE;TRUE;TRUE;FALSE;FALSE;FALSE},

MATCH(FALSE,{TRUE;TRUE;TRUE;FALSE;FALSE;FALSE},0) becomes 4; and

=NOT(ISNUMBER(4)) becomes =NOT(TRUE), which becomes FALSE.

Therefore, the data validation kicks out the value as invalid because the data validation formula is FALSE.

Let's redo this examination, with A1 containing the text Hello World:

("1:"&LEN(F1)) becomes ("1:11"))

.ROW(INDIRECT("1:11")) becomes {1;2;3;4;5;6;7;8;9;10;11}.

MID(A1,{1;2;3;4;5;6;7;8;9;10;11},1)) becomes {"H";"e";"l";"l";"o";" ";"W";"o";"r";"l";"d"})

,ISERROR(1*{"H";"e";"l";"l";"o";" ";"W";"o";"r";"l";"d"}) becomes {TRUE;TRUE;TRUE;TRUE;TRUE;TRUE;TRUE;TRUE;TRUE;TRUE;TRUE},

MATCH(FALSE,{TRUE;TRUE;TRUE;TRUE;TRUE;TRUE;TRUE;TRUE;TRUE;TRUE;TRUE},0) becomes (#N/A)).

NOT(ISNUMBER(#N/A)) becomes =TRUE.

Therefore, Hello World is a valid entry.

Making a Change in One Column Based on Criteria in Another (Without VBA)

Consider this Figure:

	A	B	C
1	Agent	Promo	Rate
2	Bob	Hotels.com	100
3	Monte	Other.com	200
4	Bonnie	Booking.com	300
5	Sue	More.com	400
6	Fred	Booking.com	100
7	Jane	Other.com	200
8	Alice	Another.com	300

Someone recently asked me how he could change the agent names in column A to "Internet" whenever column B contained either Hotels.com or Booking.com.

One way to do this would be to use a helper column: You could simply use an if-statement to test for either value and use "Internet" if TRUE or the current value in column A if FALSE; then you would copy the helper column and paste values into column A and then clear the helper column.

But this person didn't want to use a helper column—or VBA.

I thought about the problem a bit and came up with another way to approach it. I added a filter to the range and then select Hotels.com and Booking.com from column B:

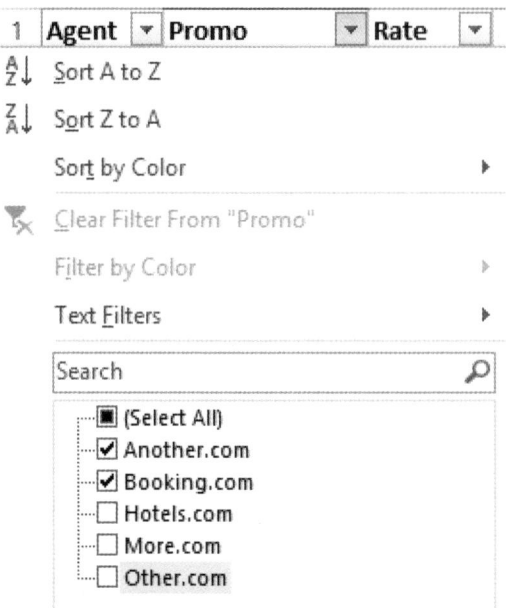

This yields the following:

	A	B	C
1	Agent ▼	Promo ⊤	Rate ▼
2	Bob	Hotels.com	100
4	Bonnie	Booking.com	300
6	Fred	Booking.com	100
9	Jim	Hotels.com	400

Next, I selected from A2 to the bottom and pressed Alt+; (the equivalent of se-lecting Go To Special/Visible Cells Only):

	A	B	C
1	Agent ▼	Promo ⊤	Rate ▼
2	Bob	Hotels.com	100
4	Bonnie	Booking.com	300
6	Fred	Booking.com	100
9	Jim	Hotels.com	400

Next, I typed Internet and pressed Ctrl+Enter:

	A	B	C
1	Agent ▼	Promo ⊤	Rate ▼
2	Internet	Hotels.com	100
4	Internet	Booking.com	300
6	Internet	Booking.com	100
9	Internet	Hotels.com	400

When I cleared the filter, I saw that I was done:

	A	B	C
1	Agent ▼	Promo ▼	Rate ▼
2	Internet	Hotels.com	100
3	Monte	Other.com	200
4	Internet	Booking.com	300
5	Sue	More.com	400
6	Internet	Booking.com	100
7	Jane	Other.com	200
8	Alice	Another.com	300
9	Internet	Hotels.com	400

Changing Row Height When a Key Field Changes

Look at this figure, which is part of a worksheet that continues for hundreds of rows:

	A	B	C	D	E	F
1	QUADRANT	DISTRICT	UNIT	TERRITORY	RTLACCT	NAME
2						
3	1	2271	2201	220101	790340	JOHN'S CHICKEN
4	2	2271	2201	220101	391422	FOOD LION
5	1	2271	2201	220101	671374	PETROLEUM WORLD EXP
6	1	2271	2201	220101	786406	SCOTTS FOOD STORE
7	1	2271	2201	220101	670796	LAKE WYLIE MARKET
8	2	2271	2201	220102	257647	QUIK SHOPPE
9	1	2271	2201	220102	312486	RAY'S QUICK SHOP
10	2	2271	2201	220102	670818	HILCREST GROCERY
11	1	2271	2201	220102	134191	WOODLAND SUPER MARKE
12	2	2271	2201	220102	389058	KERR DRUG
13	1	2271	2201	220102	284839	DRUG EMPORIUM
14	2	2271	2201	220102	538058	ECKERD DRUG
15	1	2271	2201	220102	591908	A W'S MINI MART
16	1	2271	2201	220102	739174	RITE AID
17	1	2271	2201	220103	132262	BLACKSBURG HARDWARE
18	1	2271	2201	220103	583249	CLACK'S

Say that the important column here is D, and you want to make the worksheet group together the rows with the same territory field, like this:

	A	B	C	D	E	F
1	QUADRANT	DISTRICT	UNIT	TERRITORY	RTLACCT	NAME
2						
3	1	2271	2201	220101	790340	JOHN'S CHICKEN
4	2	2271	2201	220101	391422	FOOD LION
5	1	2271	2201	220101	671374	PETROLEUM WORLD EXP
6	1	2271	2201	220101	786406	SCOTTS FOOD STORE
7	1	2271	2201	220101	670796	LAKE WYLIE MARKET
8	2	2271	2201	220102	257647	QUIK SHOPPE
9	1	2271	2201	220102	312486	RAY'S QUICK SHOP
10	2	2271	2201	220102	670818	HILCREST GROCERY
11	1	2271	2201	220102	134191	WOODLAND SUPER MARKE
12	2	2271	2201	220102	389058	KERR DRUG
13	1	2271	2201	220102	284839	DRUG EMPORIUM
14	2	2271	2201	220102	538058	ECKERD DRUG
15	1	2271	2201	220102	591908	A W'S MINI MART
16	1	2271	2201	220102	739174	RITE AID
17	1	2271	2201	220103	132262	BLACKSBURG HARDWARE
18	1	2271	2201	220103	583249	CLACK'S

In this case, rows 8 and 17 have a different height than the other rows, which provides some visual grouping for the territory entries.

To accomplish this kind of grouping, you can use a simple formula. In cell G4, you use the following formula:

| ✕ | ✓ | *fx* | =IF(D3<>D4,1,NA()) |

D	E	F	G
TERRITORY	**RTLACCT**	**NAME**	
220101	790340	JOHN'S CHICKEN	
220101	391422	FOOD LION	#N/A
220101	671374	PETROLEUM WORLD EXP	

(You start at row 4 because that's the first row that could be different.) Then you fill the formula down to the bottom:

	A	B	C	D	E	F	G
1	QUADRANT	DISTRICT	UNIT	TERRITORY	RTLACCT	NAME	
2							
3	1	2271	2201	220101	790340	JOHN'S CHICKEN	
4	2	2271	2201	220101	391422	FOOD LION	#N/A
5	1	2271	2201	220101	671374	PETROLEUM WORLD EXP	#N/A
6	1	2271	2201	220101	786406	SCOTTS FOOD STORE	#N/A
7	1	2271	2201	220101	670796	LAKE WYLIE MARKET	#N/A
8	2	2271	2201	220102	257647	QUIK SHOPPE	1
9	1	2271	2201	220102	312486	RAY'S QUICK SHOP	#N/A
10	2	2271	2201	220102	670818	HILCREST GROCERY	#N/A
11	1	2271	2201	220102	134191	WOODLAND SUPER MARKE	#N/A
12	2	2271	2201	220102	389058	KERR DRUG	#N/A
13	1	2271	2201	220102	284839	DRUG EMPORIUM	#N/A
14	2	2271	2201	220102	538058	ECKERD DRUG	#N/A
15	1	2271	2201	220102	591908	A W'S MINI MART	#N/A
16	1	2271	2201	220102	739174	RITE AID	#N/A
17	1	2271	2201	220103	132262	BLACKSBURG HARDWARE	1
18	1	2271	2201	220103	583249	CLACK'S	#N/A

Notice the 1s that appear in cells G8 and G17. The formula in G8 is =IF-(D7<>D8,1,NA()), and D7 is not equal to D8, hence the 1. If you now select column G and press F5 (Go To) and click Special, you see these options:

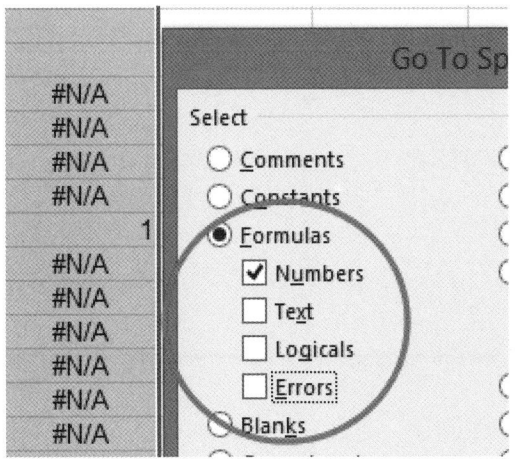

Notice that there are four sections under Formulas. Because you set up the formula to produce either a 1 or a #N/A value, you can now isolate just the numbers and ignore the errors. The original formula could have used any two of these options, though. For example, it could have used =IF(D3<>D4, "X",TRUE) to distinguish between text and logical values.

Now when you select just the formulas that are numbers, you see this:

	QUADRANT	DISTRICT	UNIT	TERRITORY	RTLACCT	NAME	
1	QUADRANT	DISTRICT	UNIT	TERRITORY	RTLACCT	NAME	
2							
3	1	2271	2201	220101	790340	JOHN'S CHICKEN	
4	2	2271	2201	220101	391422	FOOD LION	#N/A
5	1	2271	2201	220101	671374	PETROLEUM WORLD EXP	#N/A
6	1	2271	2201	220101	786406	SCOTTS FOOD STORE	#N/A
7	1	2271	2201	220101	670796	LAKE WYLIE MARKET	#N/A
8	2	2271	2201	220102	257647	QUIK SHOPPE	1
9	1	2271	2201	220102	312486	RAY'S QUICK SHOP	#N/A
10	2	2271	2201	220102	670818	HILCREST GROCERY	#N/A
11	1	2271	2201	220102	134191	WOODLAND SUPER MARKE	#N/A
12	2	2271	2201	220102	389058	KERR DRUG	#N/A
13	1	2271	2201	220102	284839	DRUG EMPORIUM	#N/A
14	2	2271	2201	220102	538058	ECKERD DRUG	#N/A
15	1	2271	2201	220102	591908	A W'S MINI MART	#N/A
16	1	2271	2201	220102	739174	RITE AID	#N/A
17	1	2271	2201	220103	132262	BLACKSBURG HARDWARE	1
18	1	2271	2201	220103	583249	CLACK'S	#N/A

As you can see, only G8 and G17 are selected. So now you can change the row height from the Format tab:

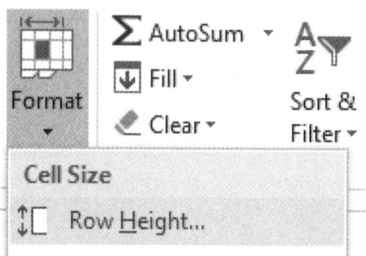

When you change the Row Height now, it applies to just those selected rows. You can set it to 25 or any other value:

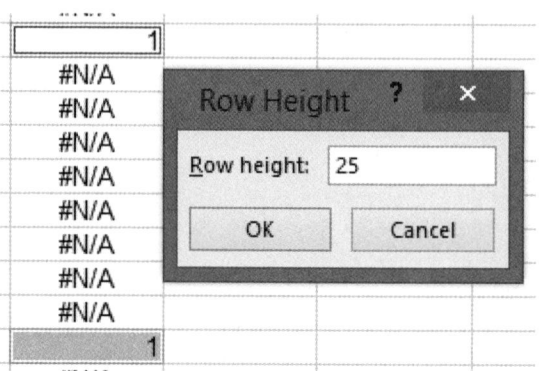

This is what you see now:

	A	B	C	D	E	F	G
1	QUADRANT	DISTRICT	UNIT	TERRITORY	RTLACCT	NAME	
2							
3	1	2271	2201	220101	790340	JOHN'S CHICKEN	
4	2	2271	2201	220101	391422	FOOD LION	#N/A
5	1	2271	2201	220101	671374	PETROLEUM WORLD EXP	#N/A
6	1	2271	2201	220101	786406	SCOTTS FOOD STORE	#N/A
7	1	2271	2201	220101	670796	LAKE WYLIE MARKET	#N/A
8	2	2271	2201	220102	257647	QUIK SHOPPE	1
9	1	2271	2201	220102	312486	RAY'S QUICK SHOP	#N/A
10	2	2271	2201	220102	670818	HILCREST GROCERY	#N/A
11	1	2271	2201	220102	134191	WOODLAND SUPER MARKE	#N/A
12	2	2271	2201	220102	389058	KERR DRUG	#N/A
13	1	2271	2201	220102	284839	DRUG EMPORIUM	#N/A
14	2	2271	2201	220102	538058	ECKERD DRUG	#N/A
15	1	2271	2201	220102	591908	A W'S MINI MART	#N/A
16	1	2271	2201	220102	739174	RITE AID	#N/A
17	1	2271	2201	220103	132262	BLACKSBURG HARDWARE	1
18	1	2271	2201	220103	583249	CLACK'S	#N/A

All that's left to do is clear column G!

Using a Nontrivial Conditional Formatting Formula

Someone asked me how to conditionally format each month's data if its value is different from the previous month's value by 10%. Handling this request doesn't sound too difficult, but there are a couple of hitches. First, the data occurs in every fourth column. Also, if there is no data for the previous month, then you need to go back to the most recent month that does have data. So if there was data for January and April, the formatting for April would be dependent on the percentage change between April and January, but if new data was "found" and put into February or March, then the same formula should be looking at the new percentage change (April vs. February or April vs. March).

Here's a small sample to work with:

▲	A	B	C	D	E	F	G	H	I	J	K	L	M	N	
1	Jan		Other	Other	Other	Feb		Other	Other	Other	Mar		Other	Other	Other	Apr	
2		1000	1054	1277	1003	1200	1176	1198	1161	1062	1094	1251	1299	1221
3															
4															
5															
6						20.0%				11.5%				15.0%	

As you can see, cell J2 (March) is highlighted because the percentage difference between it and cell F2 (February) is 11.5%. The formula in J6 is =ABS((J2-F2)/F2). However, if the February data were cleared, you'd see this:

▲	A	B	C	D	E	F	G	H	I	J	K	L	M	N
1	Jan		Other	Other	Other	Feb		Other	Other	Other	Mar		Other	Other	Other	Apr
2		1000	1054	1277	1003					1062	1094	1251	1299	1221

Now March isn't highlighted because the formula is comparing the 1062 in J2 with the value for January in B2, and that's less than 10%—because ABS((J2-B2)/B2) is 6.2%.

So what formula can you use to make this adjustment? Keep in mind that you need to be able to apply the same formula for each month through December (because January has no conditional formatting).

This Figure shows an array formula in cell J4 (which winds up being the formula used in the conditional formatting formula):

J4	▼	:	×	✓	fx	{=AND(J2<>0,ABS(J2-(INDEX($A2:I2,MAX((MOD(COLUMN($B2:I2),4)
						=2)*COLUMN($B2:I2)*($B2:I2>0)))))/(INDEX($A2:I2,MAX((MOD(
						COLUMN($B2:I2),4)=2)*COLUMN($B2:I2)*($B2:I2>0))))>0.1)}

▲	A	B	C	D	E	F	G	H	I	J	K	L	M	N	
1	Jan		Other	Other	Other	Feb		Other	Other	Other	Mar		Other	Other	Other	Apr	O
2		1000	1054	1277	1003	1200	1176	1198	1161	1062	1094	1251	1299	1221
3															
4										TRUE					

Notice here that the formula contains mixed references in the formula: It goes from A or B as absolute to I (as relative—the column just before the active cell).

The same formula in cell N4 is shown here:

| N4 | ▾ | : | ✕ | ✓ | f_x | {=AND(N2<>0,ABS(N2-(INDEX($A2:M2,MAX((MOD(COLUMN($B2:M2),4) =2)*COLUMN($B2:M2)*($B2:M2>0)))))/(INDEX($A2:M2,MAX((MOD(COLUMN($B2:M2),4)=2)*COLUMN($B2:M2)*($B2:M2>0))))>0.1)} |

◢ A	B	C	D	E	F	G	H	I	J	K	L	M	N	O
1	Jan	Other	Other	Other	Feb	Other	Other	Other	Mar	Other	Other	Other	Apr	Other
2	1000	1054	1277	1003	1200	1176	1198	1161	1062	1094	1251	1299	1221	
3														
4									TRUE				TRUE	

As you can see, it now refers from column A or B to M. It's time to decipher this to see how it works, using the formula for March in J4. You can first look at it as if there is data in February.

The first calculation involves looking only at columns B, F, J, N, etc. These columns have something in common: Their column numbers (2, 6, 10, 14, …) all give a remainder of 2 when divided by 4. They're the only columns you're interested in:

=AND(J2<>0,ABS(J2-(INDEX($A2:I2,MAX((MOD(COLUMN($B2:I2),4) =2)*COLUMN($B2:I2)*($B2:I2>0)))))/(INDEX($A2:I2,MAX((MOD(COLUMN($B2:I2),4)=2)*COLUMN($B2:I2)*($B2:I2>0))))>0.1)

This formula expands to:

=AND(J2<>0,ABS(J2-(INDEX($A2:I2,MAX(({TRUE,FALSE,FALSE, FALSE,TRUE,FALSE,FALSE,FALSE})*COLUMN($B2:I2)*($B2:I2>0)))))/(INDEX($A2:I2,MAX((MOD(COLUMN($B2:I2),4)=2)*COLUMN($B2:I2) *($B2:I2>0))))>0.1)

When you multiply this series of TRUE and FALSE values by the same column numbers, you see the following:

=AND(J2<>0,ABS(J2-(INDEX($A2:I2,MAX({2,0,0,0,6,0,0,0}*($B2:I2>0)))))/(INDEX($A2:I2,MAX((MOD(COLUMN($B2:I2),4)=2)*COLUMN($B2:I2)*($B2:I2>0))))>0.1)

Now because you're interested in this column only if there's data in it, you also multiply by the "truth" of these values containing data (also assuming only positive numbers here):

=AND(J2<>0,ABS(J2-(INDEX($A2:I2,MAX({2,0,0,0,6,0,0,0}*($B2:I2>0))))/(INDEX($A2:I2,MAX((MOD(COLUMN($B2:I2),4)=2)*COLUMN($B2:I2)*($B2:I2>0))))>0.1)

This formula expands to:

```
=AND(J2<>0,ABS(J2-(INDEX($A2:I2,MAX({2,0,0,0,6,0,0,0}))))/(
INDEX($A2:I2,MAX((MOD(COLUMN($B2:I2),4)=2)*COLUMN($B2:I2)
*($B2:I2>0))))>0.1)
```

And you want the latest column, hence the MAX, which gives 6. So now this part:

```
=AND(J2<>0,ABS(J2-(INDEX($A2:I2,MAX({2,0,0,0,6,0,0,0})))/(
INDEX($A2:I2,MAX((MOD(COLUMN($B2:I2),4)=2)*COLUMN($B2:I2)
*($B2:I2>0))))>0.1)
```

is the INDEX(A2:I2,6), or F2, or 1200:

```
=AND(J2<>0,ABS(J2-(1200))/(INDEX($A2:I2,MAX((MOD(COLUMN(
$B2:I2),4)=2)*COLUMN($B2:I2)*($B2:I2>0))))>0.1)
```

When you subtract this from J2, you get:

```
=AND(J2<>0,ABS(-138)/(INDEX($A2:I2,MAX((MOD(COLUMN($B2:I2),4)=2)*COLUMN($B2:
I2)*($B2:I2>0))))>0.1)
```

Okay, so what are you dividing the -138 by? The denominator is the same; the formula in easy terms is =ABS((J2-F2)/F2), and that 1200 from two screenshots ago is what you're after. So now you have:

```
=AND(J2<>0,ABS(-138)/INDEX($A2:I2,MAX((MOD(COLUMN($B2:I2),4)=2)*COLUMN($B2:
I2)*($B2:I2>0))))>0.1)
```

which is:

```
=AND(J2<>0,ABS(-138)/1200>0.1)
```

which is:

```
=AND(J2<>0,0.115>0.1)
```

or TRUE.

Now let's take one more look when February is blank. The inner part now expands to:

```
=AND(J2<>0,ABS(J2-(INDEX($A2:I2,MAX({2,0,0,0,0,0,0,0}))))/(INDEX($A2:I2,MAX((MOD(
COLUMN($B2:I2),4)=2)*COLUMN($B2:I2)*($B2:I2>0))))>0.1)
```

And this is the INDEX(A2:I2,2), or 1000:

=AND(J2<>0,ABS(J2-(1000))/1000>0.1)

which is:

=AND(J2<>0,0.062>0.1)

which is FALSE, so no conditional formatting.

To apply this to a whole column, you can use the Format Painter on cell F2 and then click on column F. Then you select F:I, like this:

◢ A	B	C	D	E	F	G	H	I	J	K
1	Jan	Other	Other	Other	Feb	Other	Other	Other	Mar	Other
2	1000	1054	1277	1003					1062	1094
3										

Then you right-click and drag the fill handle from the top-right corner of cell I1 to column AT (December), and when you let go, you see this:

<u>C</u>opy Cells

Fill <u>S</u>eries

Fill <u>F</u>ormatting Only

Fill With<u>o</u>ut Formatting

When you select Fill Formatting Only, you are done:

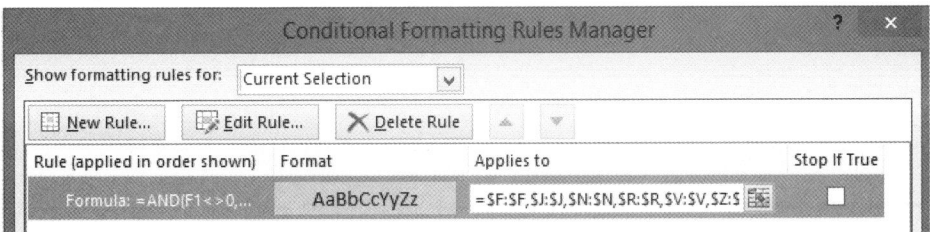

Notice that the formatting rules apply to columns F, J, N, R, V, etc.

One more screenshot:

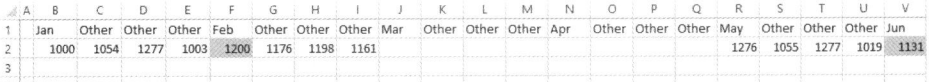

May isn't highlighted because the value in February is being compared to the 1276 for May, and that's not >10%. February and June are highlighted because the most recent month is over a 10% change.

Rearranging Data (Revisiting a Technique from Excel Outside the Box)

Someone recently ask me to help him reorganize his data from one long list into three columns. He sent me a workbook with a small sample manually started to show what he wanted:

	A	B	C	D	E
1	RIY2046		Site ID	LAT	LON
2	47		RIY2046	47	25
3	25		AFF0520	43	24
4	AFF0520				
5	43				
6	24				
7	AFF0521				
8	43				
9	24				

The list in column A went to A6123, and the worksheet included the sample in columns C:E for the first six items. The formulas supplied were pretty obvious:

C	D	E
Site ID	LAT	LON
=A1	=A2	=A3
=A4	=A5	=A6

But when you select C2:E3 and drag the fill handle, you get these formulas:

C	D	E
Site ID	LAT	LON
=A1	=A2	=A3
=A4	=A5	=A6
=A3	=A4	=A5
=A6	=A7	=A8
=A5	=A6	=A7
=A8	=A9	=A10
=A7	=A8	=A9

This clearly is not what you want. You can solve this problem in two ways: using a formula or using VBA. Let's look at them both, starting with the formula version.

Using a Formula to Rearrange Data

You can change the formulas in C2:D3 to text by using the Replace command:

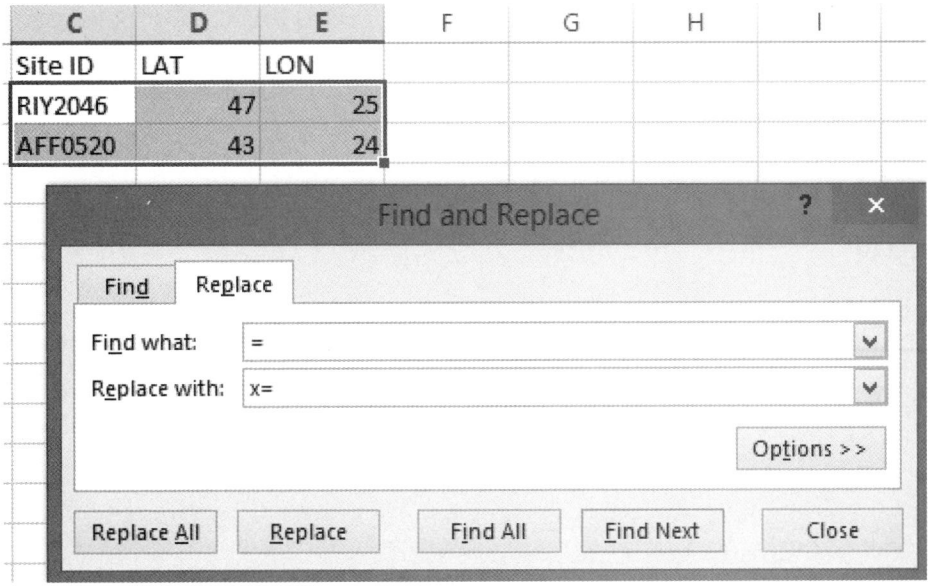

	C	D	E	F	G	H	I
	Site ID	LAT	LON				
	RIY2046	47	25				
	AFF0520	43	24				

Find and Replace ? ✕

Find | **Replace**

Find what: `=`

Replace with: `x=`

Options >>

Replace All | Replace | Find All | Find Next | Close

This yields:

	A	B	C	D	E
1	RIY2046		Site ID	LAT	LON
2	47		x=A1	x=A2	x=A3
3	25		x=A4	x=A5	x=A6
4	AFF0520				
5	43				

Now, by selecting C2:E3 and filling down a few rows, you get:

C	D	E
Site ID	LAT	LON
x=A1	x=A2	x=A3
x=A4	x=A5	x=A6
x=A7	x=A8	x=A9
x=A10	x=A11	x=A12
x=A13	x=A14	x=A15
x=A16	x=A17	x=A18

This is precisely what you need! So you can drag the fill handle down to row 2041 (that is, 6123 ÷ 3), which is a very long drag, or you can simulate the fill handle drag with a built-in but underused feature. First, you need to select C2:E2041. You can accomplish this by selecting cell C2, pressing F5 (Go To), typing E2041, and holding down the Shift key before clicking OK:

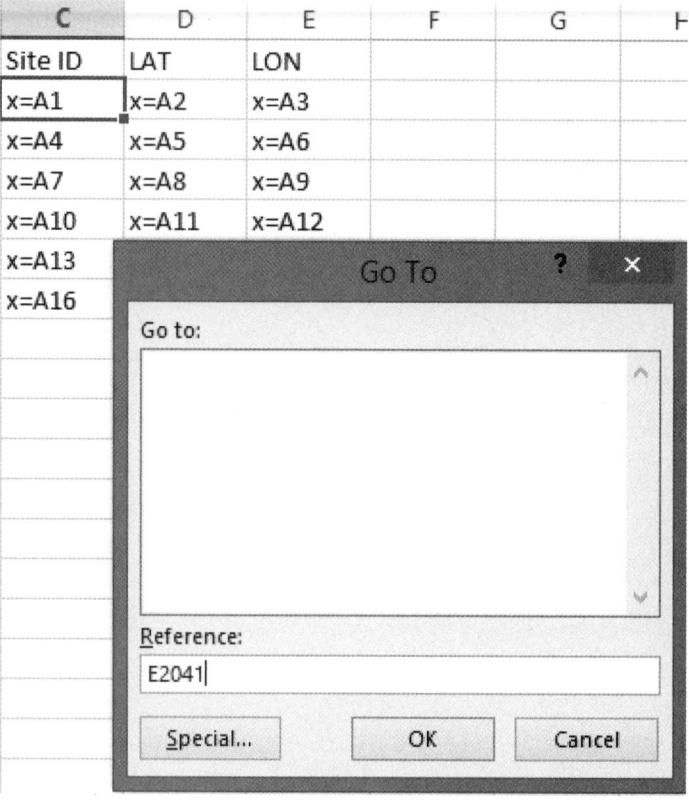

This has the effect of anchoring the active cell (C2) so the entire range C2:E2041 is now selected. At this point, you use Home/Editing/Fill/Series:

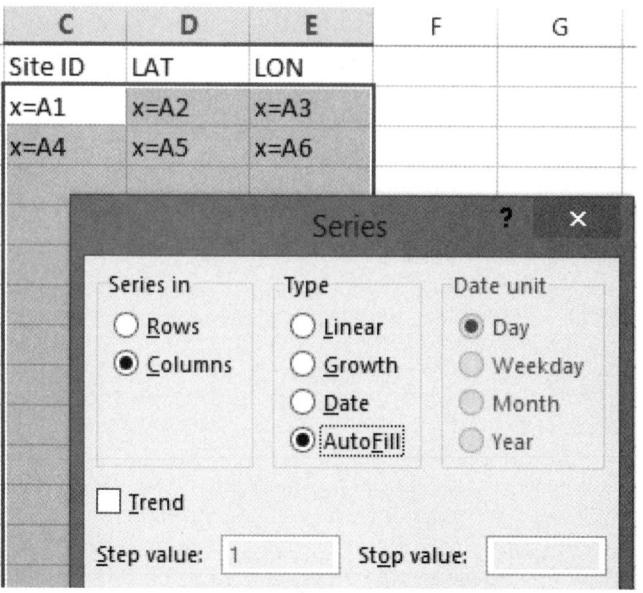

By selecting AutoFill in the Series dialog, you simulate using the fill handle:

C	D	E
Site ID	LAT	LON
x=A1	x=A2	x=A3
x=A4	x=A5	x=A6
x=A7	x=A8	x=A9
x=A10	x=A11	x=A12
x=A13	x=A14	x=A15
x=A16	x=A17	x=A18
x=A19	x=A20	x=A21
x=A22	x=A23	x=A24
x=A25	x=A26	x=A27
x=A28	x=A29	x=A30
x=A31	x=A32	x=A33
x=A34	x=A35	x=A36

Finally, you replace x= with =, and you're done:

	A	B	C	D	E
1	RIY2046		Site ID	LAT	LON
2	47		RIY2046	47	25
3	25		AFF0520	43	24
4	AFF0520		AFF0521	43	24
5	43		AFF0522	43	24
6	24		AFL0317	47	22
7	AFF0521		AFL0318	47	22
8	43		AFL0515	47	22
9	24		AQR0009	43	26
10	AFF0522		ARJ0538	44	25
11	43		ARS0143	44	26
12	24		ARS0145	43	26
13	AFL0317		ARS0171	43	25
14	47		ARS0173	43	26
15	22		ARS0174	43	26

Using VBA to Rearrange Data

The VBA approach to rearranging data is valuable, too. In VBA, if you qualify a range object with another range object, then the first one is deemed to be the entire worksheet. For example:

Range("C5:E12").Rows(3)

is the same as:

Range("C7:E7")

If C5:E12 were the entire worksheet, then the first row would be C5:E5, the second would be C6:E6, and the third would be C7:E7! In this case:

Range("C5:E12").Cells(4)

would be the same as:

Range("C6")

because after Cells(3), or (E5), the next cell would wrap to the next row. Knowing this, here's a procedure that runs very fast and creates the same result but without any formulas:

```
Sub ReFlow()
    For i = 1 To Range("A1000000").End(xlUp).Row
        Range("C2:E1000000").Cells(i).Value = Cells(i, 1).Value
    Next
End Sub
```

And here's the result:

| | C2 | ▼ | : | × | ✓ | fx | RIY2046 | |

▲	A	B	C	D	E	
1	RIY2046		Site ID	LAT	LON	
2	47		RIY2046	47	25	
3	25		AFF0520	43	24	
4	AFF0520		AFF0521	43	24	
5	43		AFF0522	43	24	
6	24		AFL0317	47	22	
7	AFF0521		AFL0318	47	22	
8	43		AFL0515	47	22	
9	24		AQR0009	43	26	
10	AFF0522		ARJ0538	44	25	
11	43		ARS0143	44	26	
12	24		ARS0145	43	26	

Let's examine the VBA code a bit more closely.

The range A1000000 is somewhat arbitrary. In this case, Range("A1000000").
End(xlup).Row would be 6123. The statement Range("C2:E1000000").Cells(i).
Value = Cells(i, 1).Value uses this range object qualified by another range object,
so C2:E1000000 is the "universe," and when i is 1, Range("C2:E1000000").
Cells(i) is cell C2. When i is 4, Range("C2:E1000000").Cells(i) is cell C3, hav-
ing "wrapped around" from cell E2. Try it; you'll like it.

Note that changing the range to six columns instead of three is trivial. The VBA
code only needs to change C2:E1000000 to C2:H1000000, and here's the new
result:

C	D	E	F	G	H
Site ID	LAT	LON			
RIY2046	47	25	AFF0520	42.90902	23.89804
AFF0521	43	24	AFF0522	42.9227	23.91354
AFL0317	47	22	AFL0318	46.7225	22.28123
AFL0515	47	22	AQR0009	43.37373	26.00958
ARJ0538	44	25	ARS0143	43.80892	25.8956
ARS0145	43	26	ARS0171	43.07023	25.494
ARS0173	43	26	ARS0174	43.18533	25.74275
ARS0175	44	25	ARS0176	43.51073	25.75906

Truncating Text and Showing an Ellipsis (…) After 47 Characters

In this Figure, you can see that cell A1 is selected, but the text shown in it is
truncated:

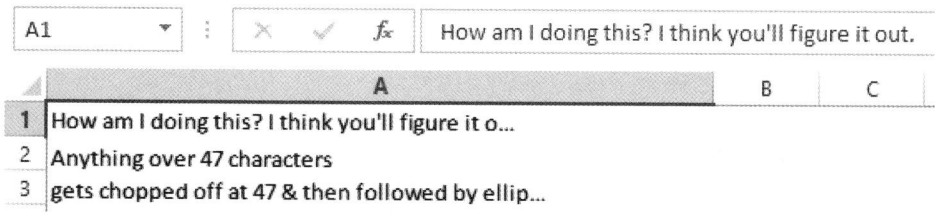

The formula bar shows the A1 text ending with "Figure it out," but the cell actually shows "Figure it o…" Why is this the case?

Now look at cell A3:

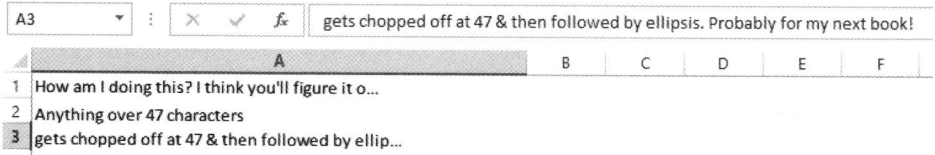

As you can see from the text in cells A2 and A3, anything over 47 characters gets chopped off and replaced by an ellipsis. What's going on? Well, a bit of trickery, of course. And it happens without macros!

Here's the length of the cells, by the way:

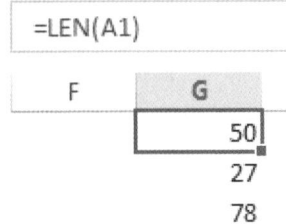

```
=LEN(A1)
```

F	G
	50
	27
	78

The trickery involves a few steps. First, let's look at column AF:

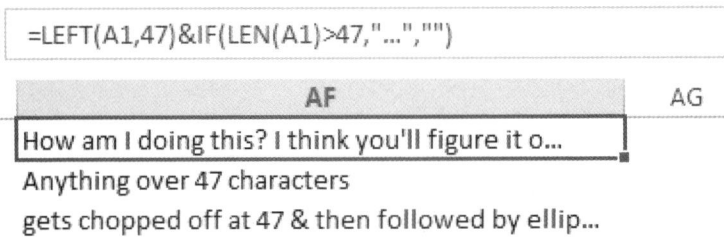

```
=LEFT(A1,47)&IF(LEN(A1)>47,"...","")
```

AF	AG
How am I doing this? I think you'll figure it o...	
Anything over 47 characters	
gets chopped off at 47 & then followed by ellip...	

The formula takes the first 47 characters in cell A1, and if there's anything after that, the formula appends the ellipsis to the first 47 characters.

As you can see here, the font color in column A is white (this is so that the picture of the text you are showing from column AF doesn't overlap with the text in column A – you'll see this in a moment):

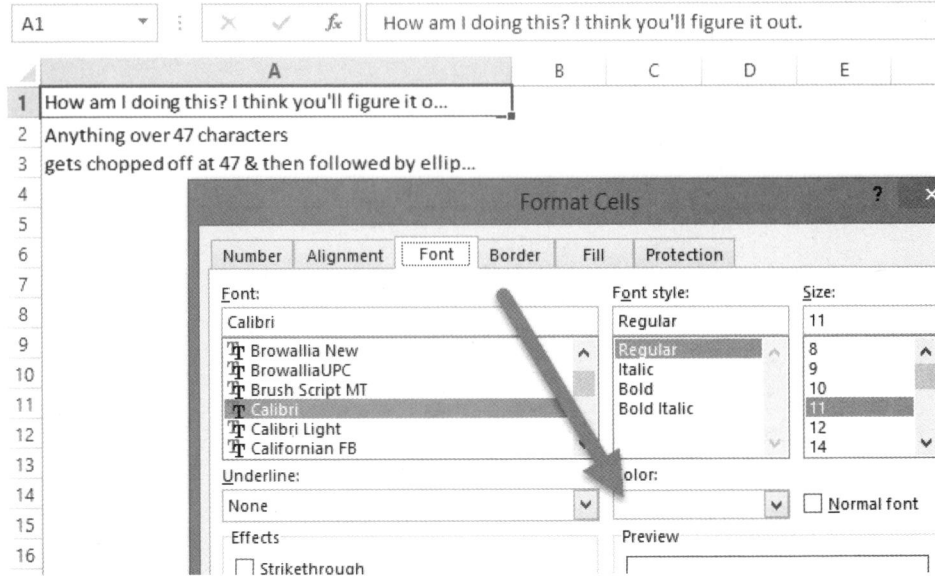

But wait! How can you see the text if it's white? To figure it out, Ctrl+click on cell A1:

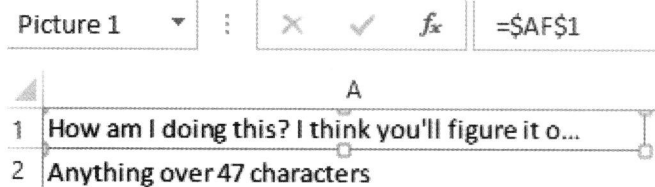

Aha! You're actually looking at a picture of the cells in column AF! To implement the trickery here, you need to use the Camera tool. You also need to make column AF the same width as column A, so the picture looks perfect, and you need to remove the border of the picture . Here's how you remove the border:

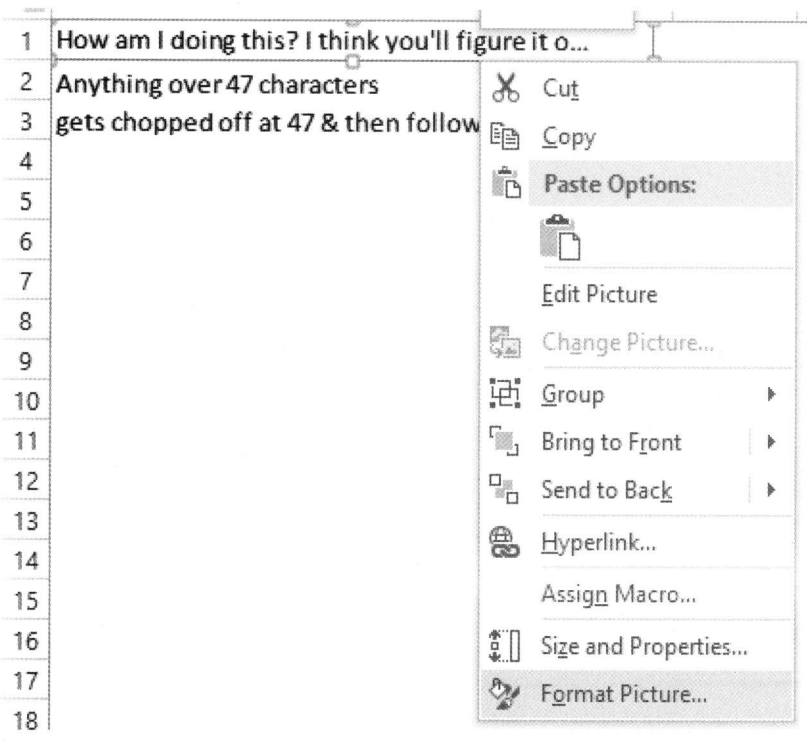

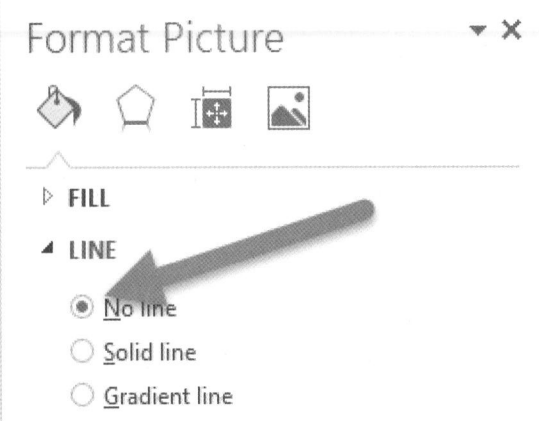

Note that this screenshot is from Excel 2013. The Format Picture options look different in other versions.

If you delete the picture, here's what you see:

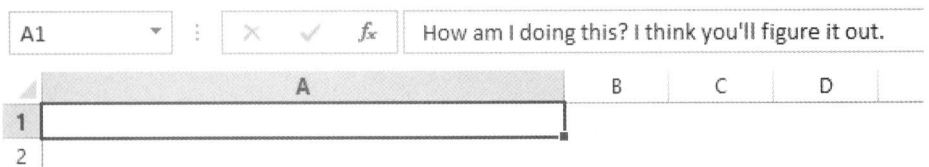

Notice that you still see the text in the formula bar, but you don't see the white font. I told you it's tricky! If it were not a white font, then both the text and the picture from column AF would show.

What? You're not sure how to use the Camera tool? You can get it by right-clicking the QAT and selecting Customize Quick Access Toolbar:

Remove from Quick Access Toolbar

Customize Quick Access Toolbar...

Show Quick Access Toolbar Below the Ribbon

Customize the Ribbon...

Collapse the Ribbon

Then you select All Commands from the top dropdown and then scroll down to the Camera tool:

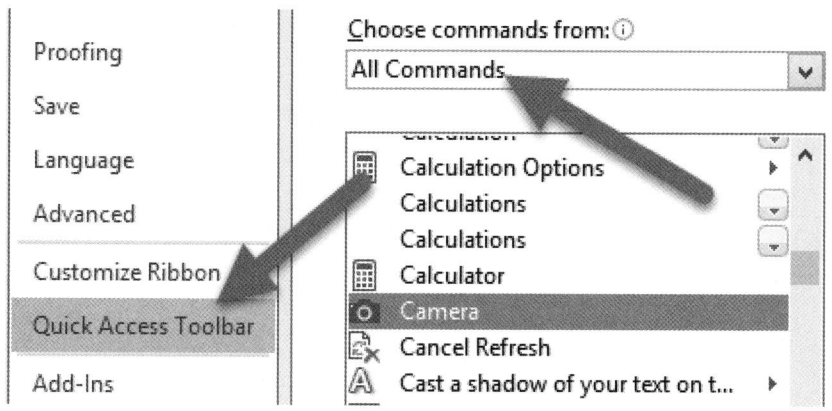

To take a picture for this example, you select AF1:AF3, click the Camera tool, then Alt+click in the top-left corner of cell A1:

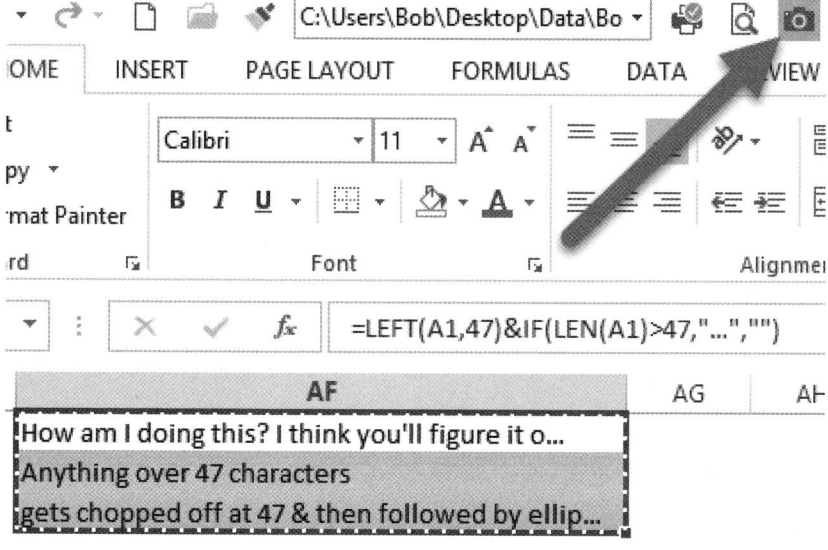

You hold down the Alt key here to align the picture with the border that's closest to where you click.

Copying Cells Without the Blank Rows

Say that you have a worksheet that looks like this:

	A	B	C
1	Text here		Copy it all here without the blank rows
2			
3			
4			
5	and here 5		
6			
7			
8			
9			
10	and here 10		
11			
12			
13	and here 13		
14	and here 14		
15			

You want it to look like this:

	A	B	C
1	Text here		Copy it all here without the blank rows
2			Text here
3			and here 5
4			and here 10
5	and here 5		and here 13
6			and here 14
7			and here 21

How do you get from point A to point B? It looks like it might be fairly difficult, but all you need to do is select all the cells containing the text, copy them, and paste them into C2. Let's walk through the process.

Select all of column A and then use the Go To Special (Press the F5 key) dialog to select Constants:

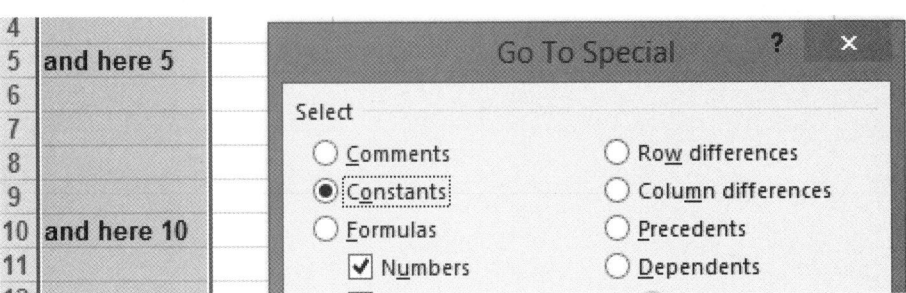

You now get this selection:

	A	B
1	Text here	
2		
3		
4		
5	and here 5	
6		
7		
8		
9		
10	and here 10	

Next, you copy. Then you select C2 and paste normally (or just press Enter). Excel puts together noncontiguous ranges by default.

If the cells you're copying contain formulas, the result after pasting will be values. Let's look at an example of this. In this case, each cell contains the formula =PI(), as you can see here in the formula bar for F3:

=PI()

D	E	F
		3.141593
		3.141593

Use the same technique as before (but this time selecting Formulas rather than Constants) and paste into cell G1:

3.14159265358979

)	E	F	G	H
			3.141593	
			3.141593	
			3.141593	
			3.141593	

Notice that the formulas are replaced by values.

Alternating Conditional Formatting

This Figure shows conditional formatting applied to weeks:

| A3 | ▼ | : | × | ✓ | *fx* | =VALUE(E1&F1) |

◢	A	B	C	D	E	F	G	H
1					March	2015		
2								
3	3/1/2015	Sun	data	data	data	data	data	data
4	3/2/2015	Mon	data	data	data	data	data	data
5	3/3/2015	Tue	data	data	data	data	data	data
6	3/4/2015	Wed	data	data	data	data	data	data
7	3/5/2015	Thu	data	data	data	data	data	data
8	3/6/2015	Fri	data	data	data	data	data	data
9	3/7/2015	Sat	data	data	data	data	data	data
10	3/8/2015	Sun	data	data	data	data	data	data
11	3/9/2015	Mon	data	data	data	data	data	data
12	3/10/2015	Tue	data	data	data	data	data	data
13	3/11/2015	Wed	data	data	data	data	data	data
14	3/12/2015	Thu	data	data	data	data	data	data
15	3/13/2015	Fri	data	data	data	data	data	data
16	3/14/2015	Sat	data	data	data	data	data	data
17	3/15/2015	Sun	data	data	data	data	data	data
18	3/16/2015	Mon	data	data	data	data	data	data

There are a few things to note here:

- Only weekday cells are highlighted; weekend cells are not.

- One week is highlighted in one color (in this case orange/pink) and the next in another (in this case green); the following week goes back to using the other color and so on.

- Cell A3 uses the VALUE function in an unusual way—in this case, VALUE(E1&F1), which is VALUE("March2015"). You might think there should be a space after the month, but the formula works fine as shown.

- Cell A4 contains =A3+1 (and is filled down).

- This technique works when you change the values in E1 and F1 (or this wouldn't be much of a tip, would it?!)

The conditional formatting formula is the same for all the cells in the range A3:H33 and is in two parts: one for the orange/pink and one for the green. The formula for green formatting is:

=AND(WEEKDAY($A3)>1,WEEKDAY($A3)<7,MOD(COUN-TIF($B$3:$B3,"Sat"),2)=1)

And the formula for orange/pink formatting is:

=AND(WEEKDAY($A3)>1,WEEKDAY($A3)<7,MOD(COUN-
TIF($B$3:$B3,"Sat"),2)=0)

The only difference between these two formulas is at the end—the 1 or 0.

The first part of both formulas ensures that the date in column A has a weekday >1 and <7—that is, Monday through Friday (WEEKDAY for a Monday date returns 2 and for a Friday returns 6). They must both be TRUE, so they're part of the AND function. Note the $ in front of the A and note that the row is relative.

The cool part of these formulas is the end:

MOD(COUNTIF($B$3:$B3,"Sat",2)=0 (or 1)

Note that the first $B$3 is absolute to cell B3, whereas the second is relative. This formula for row 3 is as shown, but for row 4, it would be MOD(COUN-TIF($B$3:$B4,"Sat",2)=0, and for row 33, it would be MOD(COUN-TIF($B$3:$B33,"Sat",2)=0. What's happening here? You're counting the number of Saturdays ("Sat") found in column B from row 3 to the current row.

Look again:

3	3/1/2015 Sun
4	3/2/2015 Mon
5	3/3/2015 Tue
6	3/4/2015 Wed
7	3/5/2015 Thu
8	3/6/2015 Fri
9	3/7/2015 Sat

In row 6, for example, the number of Saturdays from B3 to B6 is 0. The MOD(0,0) is 0, and 0 gets the orange/pink color. This is true for rows 4 through 8. In row 11, the number of Saturdays from B3 to B11 is 1. MOD(1,0) is 1, and 1 gets green. Here's a look at the MOD results in column I, where the formula in I3 is =MOD(COUNTIF($B$3:$B3,"Sat",2)):

I3	▼	:	×	✓	fx	=MOD(COUNTIF($B$3:B3,"Sat"),2)			

	A	B	C	D	E	F	G	H	I
1					March	2015			
2									
3	3/1/2015 Sun		data	data	data	data	data	data	0
4	3/2/2015 Mon		data	data	data	data	data	data	0
5	3/3/2015 Tue		data	data	data	data	data	data	0
6	3/4/2015 Wed		data	data	data	data	data	data	0
7	3/5/2015 Thu		data	data	data	data	data	data	0
8	3/6/2015 Fri		data	data	data	data	data	data	0

Using Relative Names

Look at this figure:

	A	B	C	D	E	F	G	H	I	J	K
1	Enter	Do Not Enter	Enter	Do Not Enter	Do Not Enter	Enter	Do Not Enter	Enter	Enter	Do Not Enter	Enter
2											
3											

Data for this sheet should be entered in columns A, C, F, H, I, and K, and the other columns need to be skipped. It would be nice to enter the data in column A and have it automatically jump to column C, then F, etc. You could protect the sheet and allow only unlocked cells to be selected. This method is quite valid, but it does cause some commands to become unavailable on the ribbon. You might want to avoid that restriction. Also, perhaps none of the cells were marked as locked/unlocked anyway! Can you accomplish this some other way?

If you select the cells in row 2 that are enterable, by Ctrl+clicking the columns, you probably end up with this:

B	C	D	E	F	G	H	I
lot Enter	Enter	Do Not Enter	Do Not Enter	Enter	Do Not Enter	Enter	Enter	Do N

It looks like you have to enter data in column K first. So start by selecting cell C2 first and clicking in A2 last, leaving A2 as the active cell:

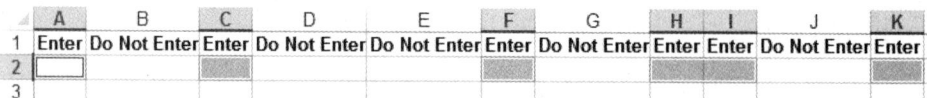

	A	B	C	D	E	F	G	H	I	J	K
1	Enter	Do Not Enter	Enter	Do Not Enter	Do Not Enter	Enter	Do Not Enter	Enter	Enter	Do Not Enter	Enter
2											
3											

Now comes the interesting part: You define a short name to be a relatively de-fined name to these columns in the next row. That is, with the above selection, if you select Define Name, you see this:

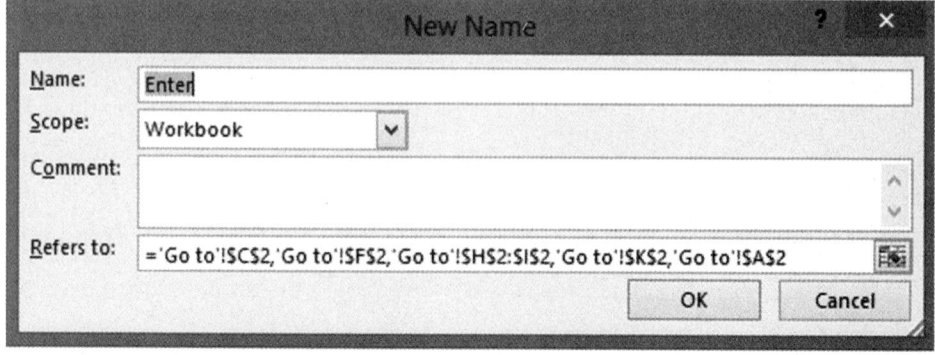

New Name	?	✕

Name: `Enter`

Scope: `Workbook` ▾

Comment: `_____`

Refers to: `='Go to'!$C$2,'Go to'!$F$2,'Go to'!$H$2:$I$2,'Go to'!$K$2,'Go to'!$A$2`

OK   Cancel

Note that Excel automatically suggests the word Enter since the active cell is next to that word in A1. Also note that 'Go to' in the Figure above represents the name of the sheet tab used for this example.

Now you change the definition and name. The following Figure shows the name changed to just the letter a:

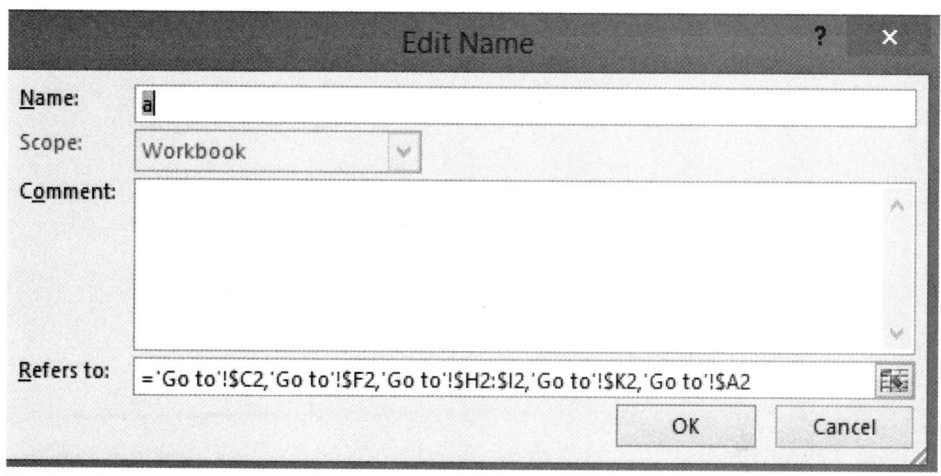

Notice that this dialog shows all the $2 references in the Refers To box changed to 3; this is a relative row reference to the next row. Look what it accomplishes:

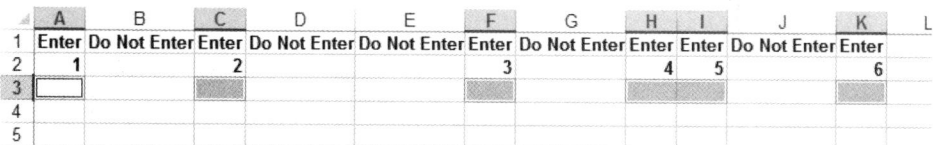

Here you enter each value and press Enter or Tab. Now you can press F5 (Go To), type a, and press Enter to get this:

	A	B	C	D	E	F	G	H	I	J	K	L
1	Enter	Do Not Enter	Enter	Do Not Enter	Do Not Enter	Enter	Do Not Enter	Enter	Enter	Do Not Enter	Enter	
2	1		2			3		4	5		6	
3												
4												
5												

You're ready to continue entering data!

Merging Across

Say that you want to merge A1:D1 as well as A2:D2 and A3:D3 and so on down to A20:D20. To handle this, you could start by merging A1:D1:

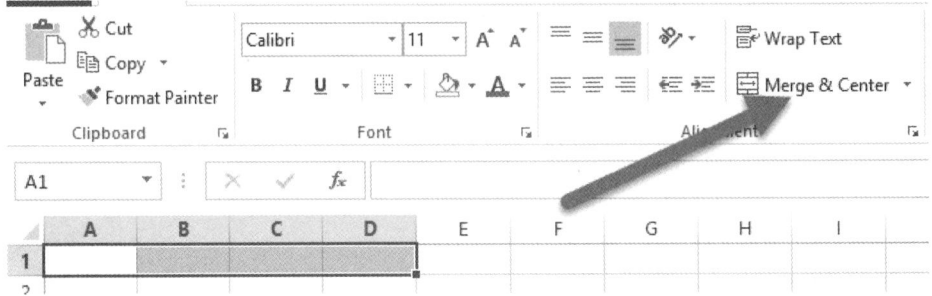

And then you would repeat this for A2:D2 and so on. But did you know there's built-in way to do this in one step in Excel? If you first select A1:D20, you can use the Merge Across command:

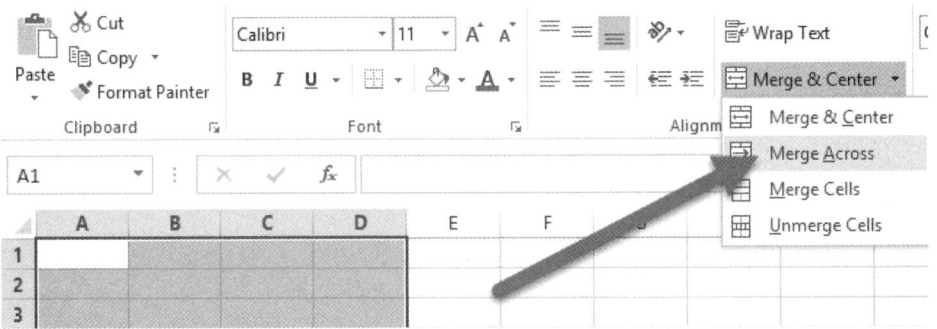

You're already done! Look:

A	B	C	D
1			
2			
3			
4			
5			
6			
7			
8			
9			
10			
11			

You can see that each row is a merged cell of four columns by one row!

Using Wildcards in Replace Formula

Suppose that in the following Figure, you only want to keep the dollar amounts in cells A1:A20 (for example, A1 should contain only $411.00, not the date):

	A
1	3/1/2014 - $411.00
2	3/2/2014 - $526.00
3	3/3/2014 - $945.00
4	3/4/2014 - $775.00
5	3/5/2014 - $26.00
6	3/6/2014 - $361.00
7	3/7/2014 $407.00

Of course, there are lots of ways to do this, but most of them involve first using a helper column. For example, you could enter this formula in B1, fill down to B20, and then copy/paste values to A1 and clear B1:B20:

B1	▼ ⋮	✕ ✓	*fx*	=MID(A1,FIND(" - ",A1)+3,100)

	A	B	C	D	E	F
1	3/1/2014 - $411.00	$411.00				
2	3/2/2014 - $526.00	$526.00				

But notice that this results in text, not formatted numbers. (You can tell because the text is left-aligned and also because the MID function returns a string.) So probably you should modify that formula to =1*MID(A1,FIND(" - ",A1)+3,100) to make it numeric. And then you need to reformat the column with $.

Another way to handle this problem is to use Flash Fill, which is new to Excel 2013. You start by entering the result you want in B2 (without any formulas):

	A	B
1	3/1/2014 - $411.00	$411
2	3/2/2014 - $526.00	$526
3	3/3/2014 - $945.00	$945
4	3/4/2014 - $775.00	$775
5	3/5/2014 - $26.00	$26
6	3/6/2014 - $361.00	$361

As you can see, as you enter the second value, Excel determines the pattern you're using and suggests in light gray the entire result. If you press Enter, you're nearly done. Because you still have a helper column, you can cut B1:B20 and paste into A1.

You can also just enter $411 in cell B1, and while B1 is selected, click Flash Fill and it also does the job!

To handle this problem without a helper column, you can use a wildcard with the Replace command:

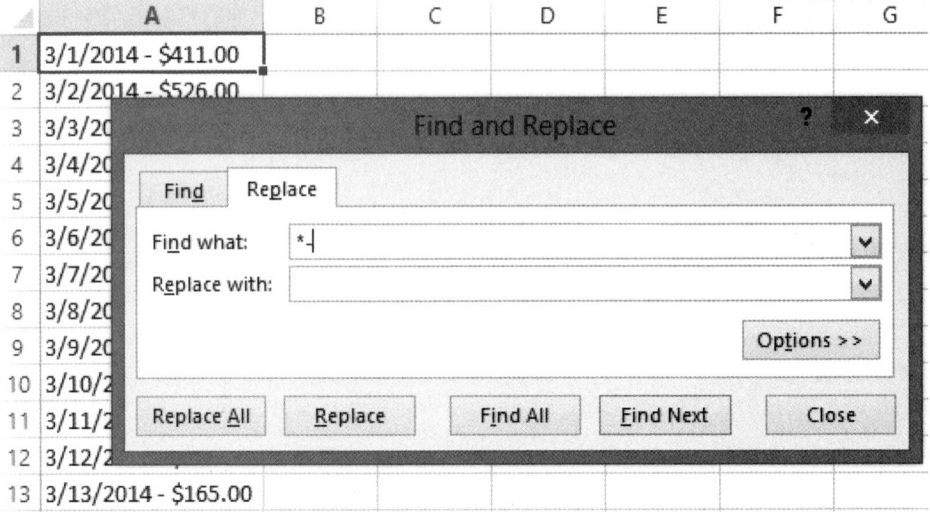

As you can see, in the Find what box, you use*- (with a trailing space). This means anything up to and including a dash followed by a space will be replaced by nothing. Here's the result:

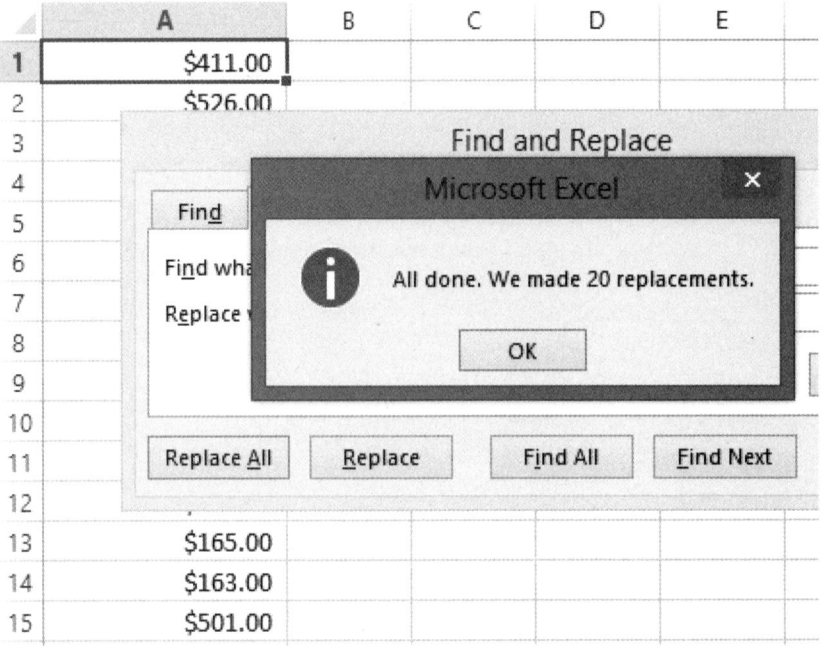

Notice that you get a formatted number, not text!

Array Formula Topics

Finding Prime Numbers

As you might remember from your school days, a prime number has no integer divisors. For example, the number 159 is divisible by 53 and 3, so it's not prime. But the number 157 has no integer divisors and it is, therefore, prime. But how can you determine whether a larger number, like 9187231, is prime? (It is.)

To Figure out if a number is prime, do you have to divide the number by all numbers less than that number? No. Clearly, if a number ends in an even number, it's not prime because it is divisible by 2. Odd numbers require more thought. Let's work with 157 to see the process. When you try to divide it by 2, you don't get an integer, so you know it's not prime. Next, you try to divide it by 3, then 4, 5, 6, etc. But you don't need to go any farther than 12. Why? Once you reach 13, the result of the division will be less than 13. What's magical about 12 or 13? The square root of 157 (~12.5) is the stopping point.

So the process (which you'll see applied in Excel in just a minute) is to divide the number by 3, 4, 5, ... , 12. If any of the results is equal to the integer value of the same results, the number 157 is not prime.

In this Figure, cell A2 contains the test value, the steps are listed in column C, and the formulas appear in column D:

	A	B	C	D
1	Test Value			
2	157		12.52996409	=SQRT(A2)
3			12	=INT(C2)
4	Prime #?		78.5	=A2/ROW(INDIRECT("2:"&C3))
5	TRUE		78	=INT(A2/ROW(INDIRECT("2:"&C3)))

First, you need the square root of 157, shown in C2. Next, you only want the integer portion of this, which is 12, in cell C3. Then you want to divide 157 by all the numbers from 2 to 12, so you use the formula =ROW(INDIRECT("2:"&C3)), which in this case is =ROW(2:12) or {2;3;4;5;6;7;8;9;10;11;12}. A2 divided by each of these numbers won't show in cell C4; only the first value shows. But all the values are there, and you can see them by pressing F2,then F9 while C4 is active:

=｛78.5;52.3333333333333;39.25;31.4;26.1666666666667;22.4285714285714;19.625;17.4444444444444;15.7;14.2727272727273;13.0833333333333｝

Cell C5 shows the same thing, but the values are truncated via the INT function:

=｛78;52;39;31;26;22;19;17;15;14;13｝

If you MATCH the values from C4 against the values from C5 by using:

MATCH(TRUE,C4-Values = C5-Values,0)

and find any TRUE value, you know the number is not prime. But if the number is prime, this MATCH would give #N/A. So you must test for this possibility by surrounding it with ISNA.

Here's the formula in A5:

{=OR(A2={2,3},ISNA(MATCH(TRUE,A2/ROW(INDIRECT("2:"&INT(SQRT(A2))))=INT(A2/ROW(INDIRECT("2:"&INT(SQRT(A2))))),0)))}

and you can see it in this figure:

A5	▾	:	×	✓	fx	{=OR(A2={2,3},ISNA(MATCH(TRUE,A2/ROW(INDIRECT("2:"&INT(SQRT(A2))))=INT(A2/ROW(INDIRECT("2:"&INT(SQRT(A2))))),0)))}					
	A	B	C	D		E	F	G	H	I
1	Test Value									
2	157		12.52996409	=SQRT(A2)						
3			12	=INT(C2)						
4	Prime #?		78.5	=A2/ROW(INDIRECT("2:"&C3))						
5	TRUE		78	=INT(A2/ROW(INDIRECT("2:"&C3)))						

Notice that this is an array formula. For the moment, you can ignore the first part of the formula, =OR(A2={2,3},...

Inside the ISNA is the MATCH formula just mentioned:

MATCH(TRUE,A2/ROW(INDIRECT("2:"&INT(SQRT(A2))))=INT(A2/ROW(INDIRECT("2:"&INT(SQRT(A2))))),0)

It matches A2/ROW(INDIRECT("2:"&INT(SQRT(A2)))) against the same thing inside INT(). That is:

A2/ROW(INDIRECT("2:"&INT(SQRT(A2)))) = INT(A2/ROW(INDIRECT("2:"&INT(SQRT(A2)))))

This is what you looked at in cells C4 and C5:

=OR(A2={2,3},ISNA(MATCH(TRUE,A2/ROW(INDIRECT("2:"&INT(SQRT(A2))))=INT(A2/ROW(INDIRECT("2:"&INT(SQRT(A2))))),0)))

Now you press F9:   =OR(A2={2,3},ISNA(#N/A))

So this is =OR(A2={2,3,TRUE}), which is TRUE, so the number is prime.

Now try the same process with the number 159:

	A	B	C	D
1	Test Value			
2	159		12.60952021	=SQRT(A2)
3			12	=INT(C2)
4	Prime #?		79.5	=A2/ROW(INDIRECT("2:"&C3))
5	FALSE		79	=INT(A2/ROW(INDIRECT("2:"&C3)))

You expand on C4 and C5:

={79.5;53;39.75;31.8;26.5;22.7142857142857;19.875;17.6666666666667;15.9;14.4545454545455;13.25}

$$=\{79;53;39;31;26;22;19;17;15;14;13\}$$

Notice that 53 exists in both arrays. So this:

`=OR(A2={2,3},ISNA(MATCH(TRUE,A2/ROW(INDIRECT("2:"&INT(SQRT(A2))))=INT(A2/ROW(INDIRECT("2:"&INT(SQRT(A2))))),0)))`

becomes this: `=OR(A2={2,3},ISNA(2))` or =OR(A2={2,3,FALSE}), which is FALSE, so the number is not prime.

Okay, why do you need the OR(A2={2,3}... part?
INDIRECT("2:"&INT(SQRT(A2))) becomes INDIRECT("2:1"), which isn't very useful! So if A2 is 2 or 3, this is TRUE, or prime.

Let's expand on the use of this powerful formula. Look at this figure:

D7			fx	=INT(RAND()*10000)								
	A	B	C	D	E	F	G	H	I	J	K	L	M
1	3953	6378	8281	1641	792	FALSE	FALSE	FALSE	FALSE	FALSE			
2	6921	5592	717	3216	8941	FALSE	FALSE	FALSE	FALSE	TRUE		SUM of primes	
3	168	7508	1805	3970	7871	FALSE	FALSE	FALSE	FALSE	FALSE		48,253	
4	9540	1582	9061	24	1279	FALSE	FALSE	FALSE	FALSE	TRUE			
5	1424	2293	774	7087	4631	FALSE	TRUE	FALSE	FALSE	FALSE			
6	6012	4624	8049	4769	4131	FALSE	FALSE	FALSE	FALSE	FALSE			
7	5607	1566	4310	7984	8247	FALSE	FALSE	FALSE	FALSE	FALSE			
8	1973	7074	2986	9421	2713	TRUE	FALSE	FALSE	TRUE	TRUE			
9	3726	815	1912	9388	1544	FALSE	FALSE	FALSE	FALSE	FALSE			
10	3082	520	7629	1448	6797	FALSE	FALSE	FALSE	FALSE	FALSE			
11	2319	7412	9784	1165	2824	FALSE	FALSE	FALSE	FALSE	FALSE			

Cells in the range A1:E18 all contain =INT(RAND()*10000). The highlighted cells are conditional formatted to highlight prime numbers. The conditional formatting formula is the same one we just looked at:

		Format only unique or duplicate values	
10	3082	▬ Use a formula to determine which cells to format	
11	2319		
12	2657	Edit the Rule Description:	
13	5039	Format values where this formula is true:	
14	8211		
15	866	=OR(A1=2,A1=3,ISNA(MATCH(TRUE,A1/ROW(INDIRECT("2:"&I	

Conditional formatting doesn't allow for curly brace formatting like OR(A1={2,3}), so it's been expanded to =OR(A1=2,A1=3,ISNA(MATCH... and it works great!

The formulas in F:J are also the same as the array-entered formula you've been looking at. In this case, F1 is array entered and filled to J18:

`{=OR(A1={2,3},ISNA(MATCH(TRUE,A1/ROW(INDIRECT("2:"&INT(SQRT(A1))))=INT(A1/ROW(INDIRECT("2:"&INT(SQRT(A1))))),0)))}`

	D	E	F	G	H	I	J	K	L	M	N	O
	1641	792	FALSE	FALSE	FALSE	FALSE	FALSE					
	3216	8941	FALSE	FALSE	FALSE	FALSE	TRUE		SUM of primes			

Finally, the formula in L3 is a simple one:

=SUMIF(F1:J18,TRUE,A1:E18)

Easily Clearing an Array-Entered Block of Cells

Look at this figure, which shows a simple multiplication table:

| B2 | ▼ | : | × | ✓ | *fx* | {=B1:H1*A2:A8} |

◢	A	B	C	D	E	F	G	H
1	Mult	1	2	3	4	5	6	7
2	1	1	2	3	4	5	6	7
3	2	2	4	6	8	10	12	14
4	3	3	6	9	12	15	18	21
5	4	4	8	12	16	20	24	28
6	5	5	10	15	20	25	30	35
7	6	6	12	18	24	30	36	42
8	7	7	14	21	28	35	42	49

You can create this table by first selecting B2:H8 and entering =B1:H1*A2:A8 via Ctrl+Shift+Enter. Entering it this way has a small advantage: It means you don't have to think about where the $ goes in the reference (which would be =B$1*$A2) as you enter it in cell B2 and then fill right and down to H8. (Instead, you could first select B2:H8 and Ctrl+Enter =B$1*$A2 rather than use Ctrl+-Shift+Enter.) If you try to clear cell B2, you get this familiar warning:

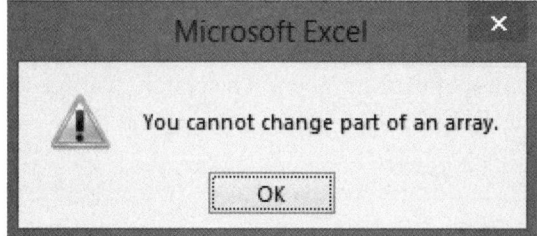

To clear this array, you usually have to first select B2:H8 and then press the Delete key or use the Clear command in the Editing group of the Home tab. For a very long array, you could select the array by using Go To Special/Current Array (or pressing Ctrl+/). But you can also clear this array by selecting any one cell in the array, pressing the Backspace key, and entering the now-blank cell with Ctrl+Shift+Enter!

Determining Whether a Cell Contains a Word from a List of Words

In this figure, column B returns TRUE when any word in column A (in the same row) exists in a list of words (in this case, C2:C8, defined as List):

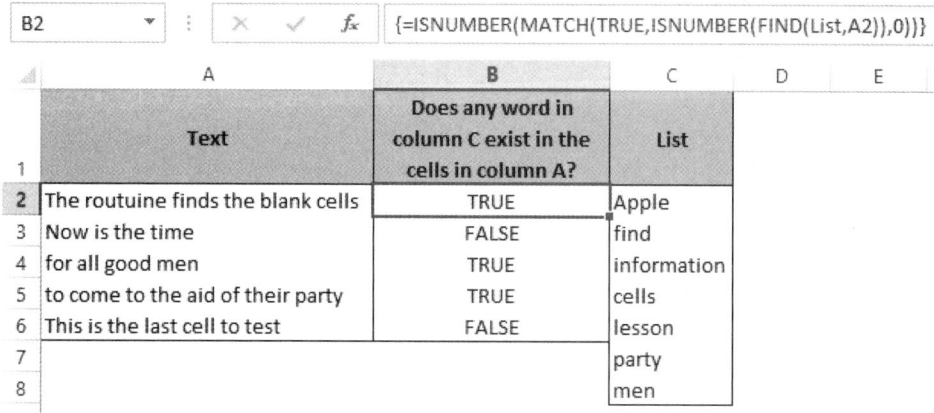

You can see that there's an array formula in cell B2, filled down to B6, and you'll see how this works. You know it's an array function because the FIND function usually takes a single value to search in a single range:

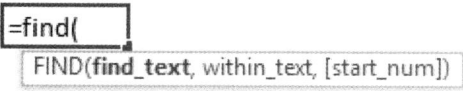

But here List is an array of values. So if you don't enter it as an array function, you get erroneous values (that is, the values in column B will all be FALSE).

So let's look at this part of the function:

=ISNUMBER(MATCH(TRUE,ISNUMBER(FIND(List,A2)),0))

Pressing F9 shows this:

=ISNUMBER(MATCH(TRUE,ISNUMBER({#VALUE!;14;#VALUE!;30;#VALUE!;#VALUE!;#VALUE!}),0))

Passing this to the ISNUMBER function:

=ISNUMBER(MATCH(TRUE,ISNUMBER({#VALUE!;14;#VALUE!;30;#VALUE!;#VALUE!;#VALUE!}),0))

yields this:

=ISNUMBER(MATCH(TRUE,{FALSE;TRUE;FALSE;TRUE;FALSE;FALSE;FALSE},0))

All the #VALUE! errors became FALSE because they're not numeric. So now, in the above, you're matching TRUE against this array because any TRUE value indicates a match from the list. This gives you:

=ISNUMBER(MATCH(TRUE,{FALSE;TRUE;FALSE;TRUE;FALSE;FALSE;FALSE},0))

or: =ISNUMBER(2)   or TRUE.

Using Variable Ranges for Unique Counts

Say that you want to be able to count unique items from a list, but with a twist. And say you're working with this worksheet:

A	B	C	D
Title	**Section**	**#Unique**	**Count**
11129 - 100 NORTH BROADWAY	ARG	8	10
11132 - ANDERSON ROBERT	ARG		
11148 - EASE RIVER CENTER LLC	ARG		
11151 - FAITH CHRISTIAN ACADE	ARG		
11157 - HUEGERICH JAMES	ARG		
11158 - EZRA A	ARG		
11158 - EZRA B	ARG		
11158 - JUNIOR LEAGUE OF MANA	ARG		
11160 - FRUIT OF THE SPIRIT H	ARG		
11179 - SUPPES TERRY L	ARG		
11145 - COMBINED CROUP LLC	BRD	3	5
11145 - PACIFIC EXPRESS STABL	BRD		
11171 - PENMEN DEVELOPMENT	BRD		
11173 - REGENT GROUP LLC	BRD		
11173 - REGENT GROUP LLC	BRD		
11142 - CANAAN MISSIONARY BAP	CLOSED	7	11
11142 - DAHLGREN KENNETH	CLOSED		
11147 - DUE UOMINI GRASSI	CLOSED		
11166 - NOB HILL REAL ESTATE	CLOSED		
11166 - RICE JO ANN	CLOSED		
11166 - Roslyn Development	CLOSED		
11183 - CORBETT AUTO BROKERS	CLOSED		
11183 - CORBETT WILLIAM J	CLOSED		
11191 - Cornerstone Contracti	CLOSED		
11194 - Duff Wapinski Ranch L	CLOSED		
11201 - Wayne Nasi Developmen	CLOSED		

Column D counts the number of rows in each of the sections from column B, and column C counts the number of unique sections based on the first five characters of column A for that section. Cells B2:B11 contain ARG, and you can count eight unique items in the first five characters of A2:A11 because A7:A9 each contain 11158, so the two duplicates are not counted. Similarly, the 5 in D12 tells you there are five rows for BRD, but within rows 12:16, there are three unique items of the first five characters, since 11145 is repeated and 11173 is repeated.

But how do you tell Excel to do this? And what formula could you use in C2 that could be copied to C12 and C17?

The simple counting formula in D2, =COUNTIF(B:B,B2), counts the number of times B2 (ARG) exists in column B.

You use a helper column to isolate the first five characters of column A, as in this figure:

F2	▼	:	✕	✓	fx	=LEFT(A2,5)

◢	A	B	C	D	E	F
1	Title	Section	#Unique	Count		First 5
2	11129 - 100 NORTH BROADWAY	ARG	8	10		11129
3	11132 - ANDERSON ROBERT	ARG				11132
4	11148 - EASE RIVER CENTER LLC	ARG				11148
5	11151 - FAITH CHRISTIAN ACADE	ARG				11151
6	11157 - HUEGERICH JAMES	ARG				11157
7	11158 - EZRA A	ARG				11158
8	11158 - EZRA B	ARG				11158
9	11158 - JUNIOR LEAGUE OF MANA	ARG				11158
10	11160 - FRUIT OF THE SPIRIT H	ARG				11160
11	11179 - SUPPES TERRY L	ARG				11179

Next, you need to somehow indicate that for ARG, you're only interested in cells F2:F11 to find the number of unique items. In general, you would find this value by using the array formula shown in this figure:

C3	▼	:	✕	✓	fx	{=SUM(1/COUNTIF(F2:F11,F2:F11))}

◢	A	B	C	D	E
1	Title	Section	#Unique	Count	
2	11129 - 100 NORTH BROADWAY	ARG	8	10	
3	11132 - ANDERSON ROBERT	ARG	8		

You use cell C3 temporarily just to show the formula; you can see that it's not present in C3 in previous figures. (You'll learn shortly how this formula works.)

So what's the formula in C2, C12, and C17? The surprising (and cool) answer is shown in this figure:

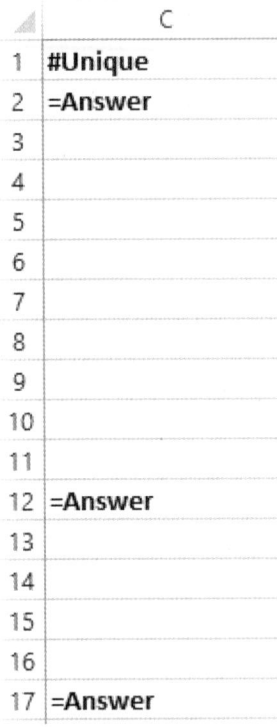

Whoa! How does this work?

Take a look at Answer in the defined names in this figure:

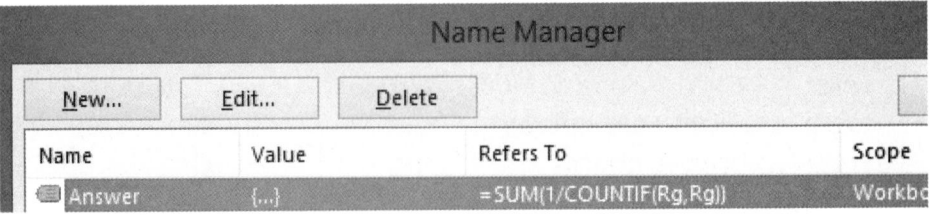

It's the same formula from an earlier figure, but instead of using the range F2:F11, it uses a range named Rg. Also, the formula was an array formula, but named formulas are treated as if they are array formulas! That is, =Answer is not entered with Ctrl+Shift+Enter but is simply entered as usual.

So how is Rg defined? If cell C1 is selected (which is an important step for understanding this trick), then it's defined as in this figure:

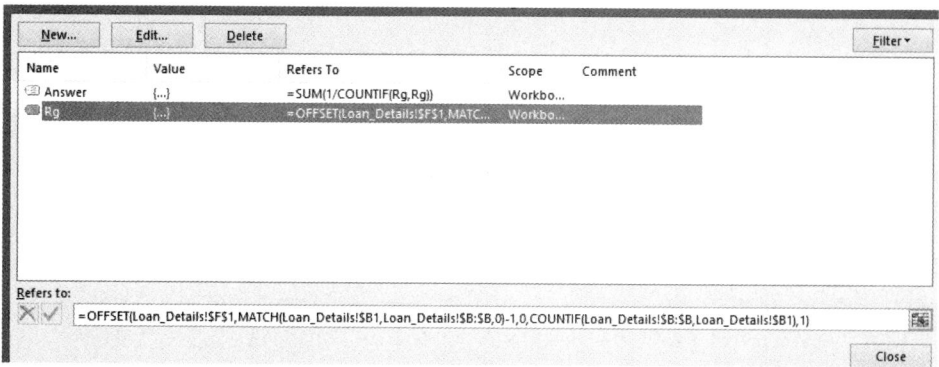

That's =OFFSET(Loan_Details!$F$1,MATCH(Loan_Details!$B1,Loan_De-tails!$B:$B,0)-1,0,COUNTIF(Loan_Details!$B:$B,Loan_Details!$B1),1).

Loan_Details is the name of the sheet, but you can look at this formula without the long sheet name. An easy way to do this is to temporarily name the sheet something simple, like x, and then look again at the defined name:

This formula is easier to read!

You can see that this formula matches $B1 (note the relative reference to the current row) against all of column B and subtracts 1. You subtract 1 because you're using OFFSET from F1. Now that you know about the formula for C, take a look at the one for C2:

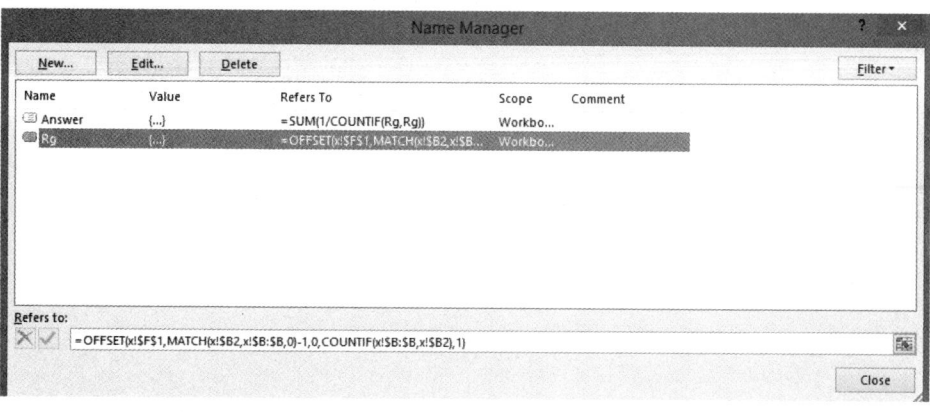

The MATCH($B2,$B:$B,0) part of the formula is 2, so the formula (without the reference to the sheet name) is:

=OFFSET($F$1,2-1,0,COUNTIF($B:$B,$B2),1)

or:

=OFFSET($F$1,1,0,COUNTIF($B:$B,$B2),1)

or:

=OFFSET($F$1,1,0,10,1)

Because COUNTIF($B:$B,$B2) is 10, there are 10 ARGs. This is range F2:F11.
As a matter of fact, if cell C2 is selected and you press F5 to go to Rg, you see
this:

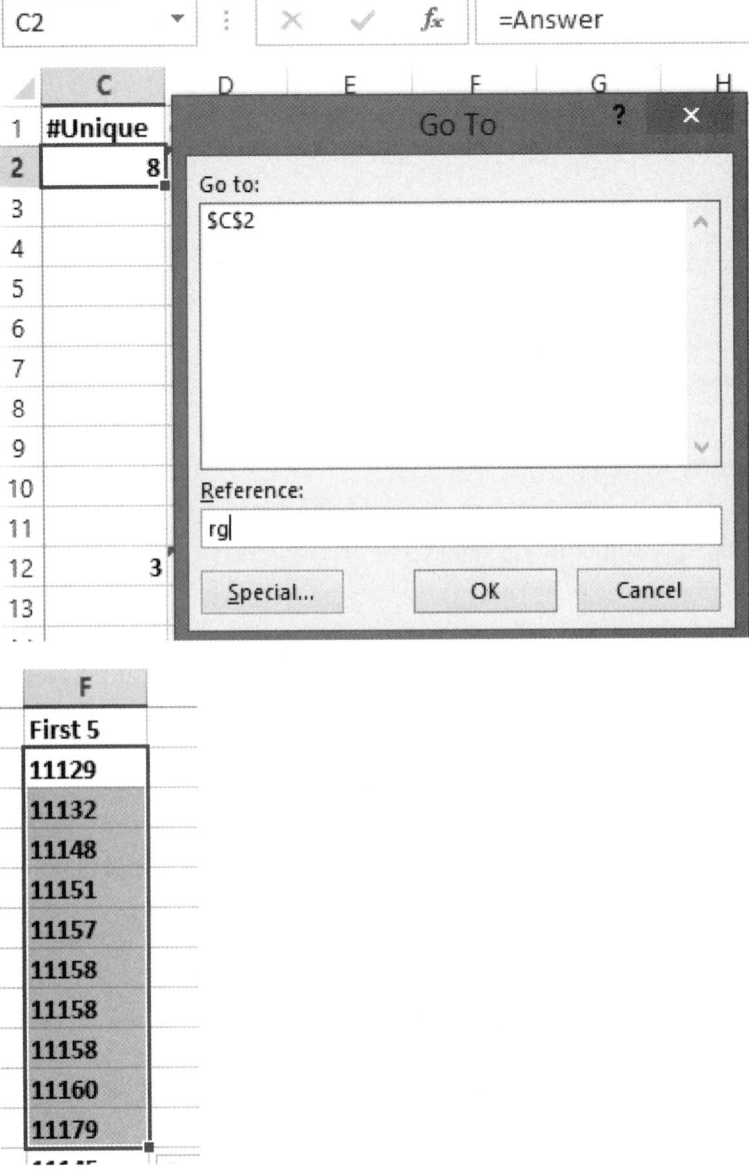

If the starting cell were C12, pressing F5 to go to Rg produces this:

▲	E	F
10		**11160**
11		11179
12		11145
13		11145
14		11171
15		11173
16		11173
17		11142

So now, with Answer defined as =SUM(1/COUNTIF(rg,rg)), you're all done!

Let's look more closely at how this formula works, using a much simpler example. Normally, the syntax for COUNTIF is =COUNTIF(range,criteria), such as =COUNTIF(C1:C10, "b") in this figure:

E1	▼	⋮	✕	✓	*fx*	{=SUM(1/COUNTIF(C1:C10,C1:C10))}

▲	A	B	C	D	E	F	G
1			a		4		
2			b				
3			b				
4			c				
5			c				
6			c				
7			d				
8			d				

This would give 2 as the number of b's in the range. But passing the range itself as the criteria uses each item in the range as the criteria. If you highlight this portion of the formula:

=SUM(1/COUNTIF(C1:C10,C1:C10))

and press F9, you see:

=SUM(1/{1;2;2;3;3;3;4;4;4;4})

Each item in the range is evaluated, and this series of numbers means there's one a and there are two b's, three c's, and four d's. These numbers are divided into 1, giving 1, ½, ½, ⅓, ⅓, ⅓, ¼, ¼, ¼, ¼, as you can see here:

=SUM({1;0.5;0.5;0.333333333333333;0.333333333333333;0.333333333333333;0.25;0.25;0.25;0.25})

So you have 2 halves, 3 thirds, 4 fourths, and 1 whole, and adding them up yields

4. If an item were repeated 7 times, then you'd have 7 sevenths and so on. Pretty cool! (Hats off to David Hager for discovering/inventing this formula.)

But hold on a minute. As it stands, you have to only enter this formula in C2, C12, and C17. Wouldn't it be better if you could enter it in C2 and fill down and only show it in the correct cells? In fact, you can do this. You can modify the formula in C2 to be =IF(B1<>B2,Answer,""), and when you fill that down, it does the job:

C2	▼	⋮	✕	✓	f_x	=IF(B1<>B2,Answer,"")		

◢	A	B	C	D	E
1	Title	Section	#Unique	Count	
2	11129 - 100 NORTH BROADWAY	ARG	8	10	
3	11132 - ANDERSON ROBERT	ARG			
4	11148 - EASE RIVER CENTER LLC	ARG			
5	11151 - FAITH CHRISTIAN ACADE	ARG			
6	11157 - HUEGERICH JAMES	ARG			
7	11158 - EZRA A	ARG			
8	11158 - EZRA B	ARG			
9	11158 - JUNIOR LEAGUE OF MANA	ARG			
10	11160 - FRUIT OF THE SPIRIT H	ARG			
11	11179 - SUPPES TERRY L	ARG			
12	11145 - COMBINED CROUP LLC	BRD	3	5	

But why stop here? Why not make the formula into a named formula, as shown here:

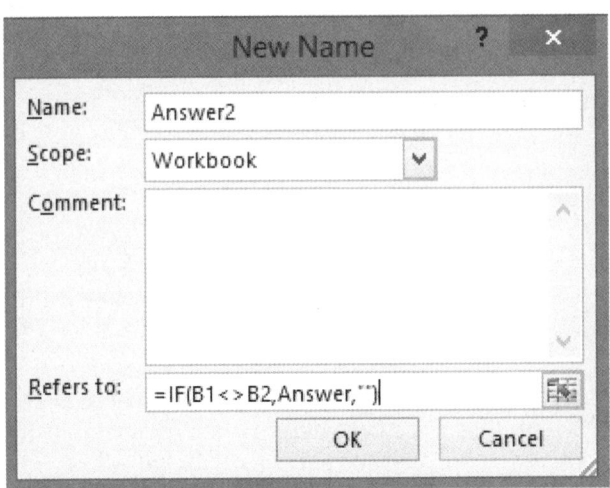

For this to work, cell C2 must be the active cell (or the formula would need to be different). Now you can replace column C's formulas with =Answer2:

C3	▼	⋮	✕	✓	*fx*	=Answer2

◢	A	B	C	C
1	Title	Section	#Unique	Coun
2	11129 - 100 NORTH BROADWAY	ARG	8	
3	11132 - ANDERSON ROBERT	ARG		
4	11148 - EASE RIVER CENTER LLC	ARG		
5	11151 - FAITH CHRISTIAN ACADE	ARG		
6	11157 - HUEGERICH JAMES	ARG		

You can see that C3 has =Answer2, as do all the cells in column C. Why not continue this in column D? The formula in D2, after also applying the comparison to B1 and B2, is shown here:

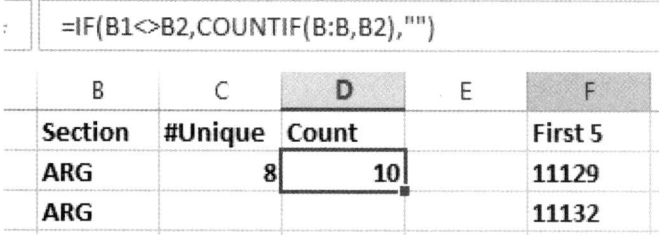

```
=IF(B1<>B2,COUNTIF(B:B,B2),"")
```

B	C	D	E	F
Section	#Unique	Count		First 5
ARG	8	10		11129
ARG				11132

So if you keep cell D2 selected and define another formula, say Answer3:

```
=IF(B1<>B2,COUNTIF(B:B,B2),"")
```

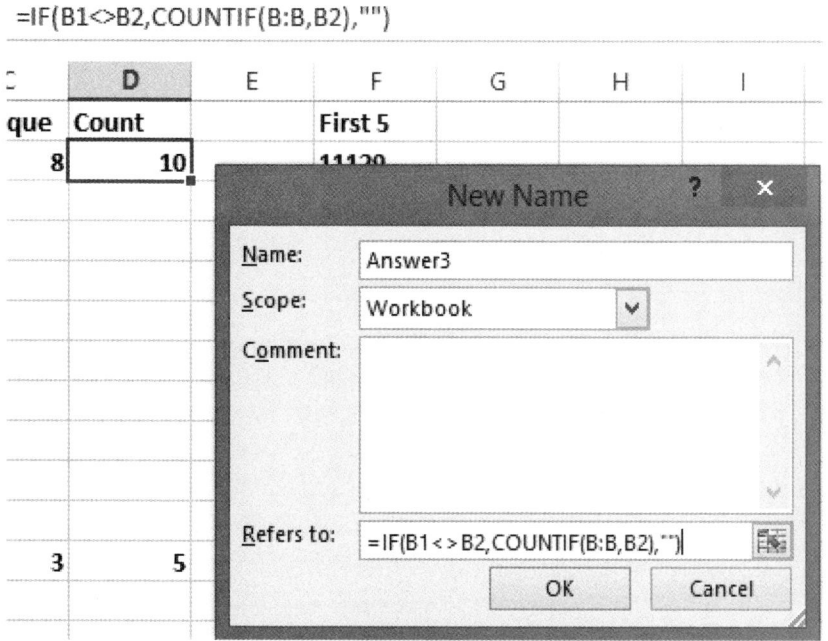

then you can enter =Answer3 in cell D2 and fill down:

| ✓ | fx | =Answer3 |

	B	C	D	E
	Section	#Unique	Count	
)WAY	ARG		8	10
₹T	ARG			
ᴘ ᴜ ᴄ	ᴀ ᴘ ᴄ			

Here's the top part of the worksheet, with formulas showing, followed by the same screenshot with values showing:

	A	B	C	D
1	Title	Section	#Unique	Count
2	11129 - 100 NORTH BROADWAY	ARG	=Answer2	=Answer3
3	11132 - ANDERSON ROBERT	ARG	=Answer2	=Answer3
4	11148 - EASE RIVER CENTER LLC	ARG	=Answer2	=Answer3
5	11151 - FAITH CHRISTIAN ACADE	ARG	=Answer2	=Answer3
6	11157 - HUEGERICH JAMES	ARG	=Answer2	=Answer3
7	11158 - EZRA A	ARG	=Answer2	=Answer3
8	11158 - EZRA B	ARG	=Answer2	=Answer3
9	11158 - JUNIOR LEAGUE OF MANA	ARG	=Answer2	=Answer3
10	11160 - FRUIT OF THE SPIRIT H	ARG	=Answer2	=Answer3
11	11179 - SUPPES TERRY L	ARG	=Answer2	=Answer3
12	11145 - COMBINED CROUP LLC	BRD	=Answer2	=Answer3
13	11145 - PACIFIC EXPRESS STABL	BRD	=Answer2	=Answer3

	A	B	C	D
1	Title	Section	#Unique	Count
2	11129 - 100 NORTH BROADWAY	ARG	8	10
3	11132 - ANDERSON ROBERT	ARG		
4	11148 - EASE RIVER CENTER LLC	ARG		
5	11151 - FAITH CHRISTIAN ACADE	ARG		
6	11157 - HUEGERICH JAMES	ARG		
7	11158 - EZRA A	ARG		
8	11158 - EZRA B	ARG		
9	11158 - JUNIOR LEAGUE OF MANA	ARG		
10	11160 - FRUIT OF THE SPIRIT H	ARG		
11	11179 - SUPPES TERRY L	ARG		
12	11145 - COMBINED CROUP LLC	BRD	3	5
13	11145 - PACIFIC EXPRESS STABL	BRD		

When other people try to figure this out, they might scratch their head at first!

Extracting Numbers from Text

As you can see in this figure, the values in column B are the digits extracted from A, expressed as numbers:

	A	B
1	4q5w6e	456
2	aaa8s9d7f	897

But how can you do this? This trick is clearly not intuitive, as you can tell from this figure:

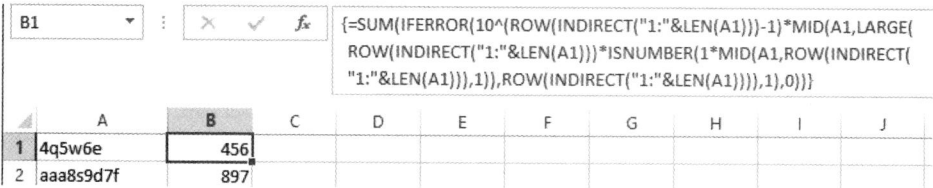

This is an excellent example of a situation where it helps to use the Evaluate Formula tool, available on the Formulas tab:

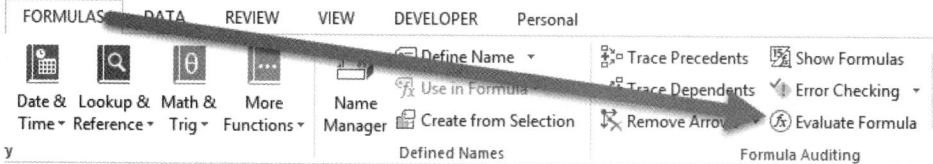

Selecting it brings up this dialog box:

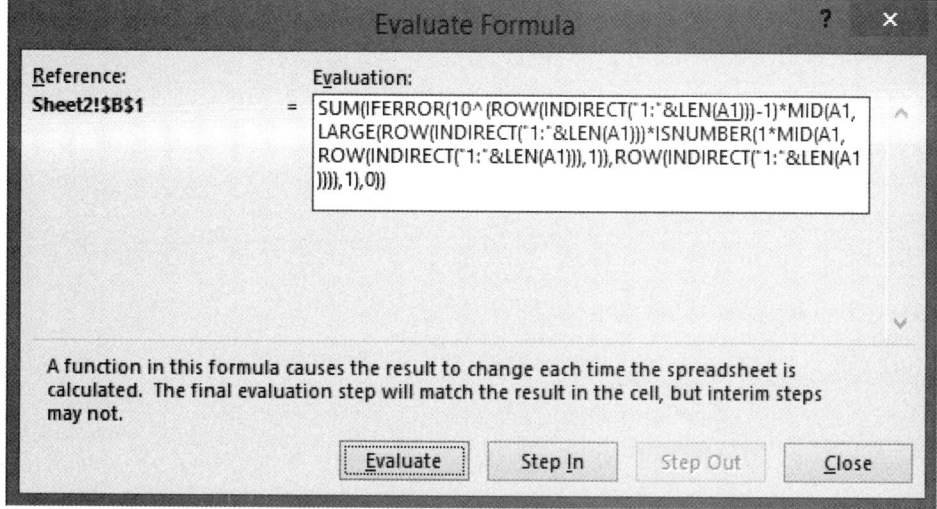

The underlined part in the figure (A1) is what's going to be evaluated next. When you click the Evaluate button, you see:

```
SUM(IFERROR(10^(ROW(INDIRECT("1:"&LEN("4g5w6e")))-1)
*MID(A1,LARGE(ROW(INDIRECT("1:"&LEN(A1)))*ISNUMBER(1
*MID(A1,ROW(INDIRECT("1:"&LEN(A1)))),1)),ROW(INDIRECT("1:"
&LEN(A1)))),1),0))
```

This figure shows the contents of A1. It also tells you that the LEN piece will be evaluated next when you click the Evaluate button again. Here's what you get then because the length is 6:

```
SUM(IFERROR(10^(ROW(INDIRECT("1:"&6))-1)*MID(A1,LARGE
(ROW(INDIRECT("1:"&LEN(A1)))*ISNUMBER(1*MID(A1,ROW
(INDIRECT("1:"&LEN(A1)))),1)),ROW(INDIRECT("1:"&LEN(A1)))),1),
0))
```

The next underlined section is evaluated, and you get:

```
SUM(IFERROR(10^(ROW(INDIRECT("1:6"))-1)*MID(A1,LARGE
(ROW(INDIRECT("1:"&LEN(A1)))*ISNUMBER(1*MID(A1,ROW
(INDIRECT("1:"&LEN(A1)))),1)),ROW(INDIRECT("1:"&LEN(A1)))),1),
0))
```

INDIRECT("1:6") effectively changes the string "1:6" into a range, meaning ROWS(1:6), as shown here (after you again click Evaluate):

```
SUM(IFERROR(10^(ROW($1:$6)-1)*MID(A1,LARGE(ROW
(INDIRECT("1:"&LEN(A1)))*ISNUMBER(1*MID(A1,ROW
(INDIRECT("1:"&LEN(A1)))),1)),ROW(INDIRECT("1:"&LEN(A1)))),1),
0))
```

Next, you get:

```
SUM(IFERROR(10^({1;2;3;4;5;6}-1)*MID(A1,LARGE(ROW
(INDIRECT("1:"&LEN(A1)))*ISNUMBER(1*MID(A1,ROW
(INDIRECT("1:"&LEN(A1)))),1)),ROW(INDIRECT("1:"&LEN(A1)))),1),
0))
```

This is a useful way to get a sequence of numbers, given a cell's contents:

ROW(INDIRECT("1:"&LEN(ref)))

You can see that this is used a number of times in this formula.

As the following text continues to expand this formula, each time it gets to the ROW(INDIRECT... part, it skips ahead to the result, {1;2;3;4;5;6}.

Next, you subtract 1 (see the -1 at the end of the evaluation), and you get: Insert

```
SUM(IFERROR(10^({0;1;2;3;4;5})*MID(A1,LARGE(ROW(INDIRECT
("1:"&LEN(A1)))*ISNUMBER(1*MID(A1,ROW(INDIRECT("1:"
&LEN(A1)))),1)),ROW(INDIRECT("1:"&LEN(A1)))),1),0))
```

The next piece is trivial—you just remove the parentheses from around the array:

```
SUM(IFERROR(10^{0;1;2;3;4;5}*MID(A1,LARGE(ROW(INDIRECT
("1:"&LEN(A1)))*ISNUMBER(1*MID(A1,ROW(INDIRECT("1:"
&LEN(A1))),1)),ROW(INDIRECT("1:"&LEN(A1)))),1),0))
```

Next, you raise 10 to the power of each number:

```
SUM(IFERROR({1;10;100;1000;10000;100000}*MID(A1,LARGE
(ROW(INDIRECT("1:"&LEN(A1)))*ISNUMBER(1*MID(A1,ROW
(INDIRECT("1:"&LEN(A1))),1)),ROW(INDIRECT("1:"&LEN(A1)))),1),
0))
```

Twelve "evaluations" later, you get this:

```
SUM(IFERROR({1;10;100;1000;10000;100000}*MID("4q5w6e",
LARGE({1;2;3;4;5;6}*ISNUMBER(1*MID("4q5w6e",{1;2;3;4;5;6},1)
),ROW(INDIRECT("1:"&LEN(A1)))),1),0))
```

This takes each character from A1 separately and multiplies by 1. Here are the next three evaluations:

```
SUM(IFERROR({1;10;100;1000;10000;100000}*MID("4q5w6e",
LARGE({1;2;3;4;5;6}*ISNUMBER(1*{"4";"q";"5";"w";"6";"e"}),ROW
(INDIRECT("1:"&LEN(A1)))),1),0))
```

```
SUM(IFERROR({1;10;100;1000;10000;100000}*MID("4q5w6e",
LARGE({1;2;3;4;5;6}*ISNUMBER({4;#VALUE!;5;#VALUE!;6;
#VALUE!}),ROW(INDIRECT("1:"&LEN(A1)))),1),0))
```

```
SUM(IFERROR({1;10;100;1000;10000;100000}*MID("4q5w6e",
LARGE({1;2;3;4;5;6}*{TRUE;FALSE;TRUE;FALSE;TRUE;FALSE},ROW
(INDIRECT("1:"&LEN(A1)))),1),0))
```

At this point, the TRUE/FALSE values are multiplied by the sequence 1 through 6. Note that you changed each #VALUE! by multiplying the alphabetic characters by 1 into FALSE values because they're not numbers. So next you get:

```
SUM(IFERROR({1;10;100;1000;10000;100000}*MID("4q5w6e",
LARGE({1;0;3;0;5;0},ROW(INDIRECT("1:"&LEN(A1)))),1),0))
```

A few evaluations later, you see this:

```
SUM(IFERROR({1;10;100;1000;10000;100000}*MID("4q5w6e",
LARGE({1;0;3;0;5;0},{1;2;3;4;5;6}), 1), 0))
```

Then you get this:

```
SUM(IFERROR({1;10;100;1000;10000;100000}*MID("4q5w6e",
{5;3;1;0;0;0}, 1), 0))
```

Note that the LARGE function uses the array {1;2;3;4;5;6} to take the largest value from the array {1;0;3;0;5;0}, which is 5. Then the second-largest value is 3, and then 5, followed by the three zeros. You're almost there! Next is:

```
SUM(IFERROR({1;10;100;1000;10000;100000}*{"6";"5";"4";
#VALUE!;#VALUE!;#VALUE!}, 0))
```

This is getting exciting. Next you multiply the two arrays together:

```
SUM(IFERROR({6;50;400;#VALUE!;#VALUE!;#VALUE!}, 0))
```

You can already see the 456 coming together! Next is:

```
SUM({6;50;400;0;0;0})
```

Each #VALUE! turned to 0 because of the IFERROR! Finally, you get the result:

```
456
```

Notice that the Evaluate button changed to Restart because you're done!

Here are the relevant Evaluation screenshots for cell B2:

```
SUM(IFERROR(10^(ROW(INDIRECT("1:"&LEN(A2)))-1)*MID(A2,
LARGE(ROW(INDIRECT("1:"&LEN(A2)))*ISNUMBER(1*MID(A2,
ROW(INDIRECT("1:"&LEN(A2))),1)),ROW(INDIRECT("1:"&LEN(A2
)))),1),0))
```

```
SUM(IFERROR(10^({1;2;3;4;5;6;7;8;9}-1)*MID(A2,LARGE(ROW
(INDIRECT("1:"&LEN(A2)))*ISNUMBER(1*MID(A2,ROW
(INDIRECT("1:"&LEN(A2))),1)),ROW(INDIRECT("1:"&LEN(A2)))),1),
0))
```

```
SUM(IFERROR({1;10;100;1000;10000;100000;1000000;10000000;
100000000}*MID(A2,LARGE(ROW(INDIRECT("1:"&LEN(A2)))
*ISNUMBER(1*MID(A2,ROW(INDIRECT("1:"&LEN(A2))),1)),ROW
(INDIRECT("1:"&LEN(A2)))),1),0))
```

```
SUM(IFERROR({1;10;100;1000;10000;100000;1000000;
10000000;100000000}*MID("aaa8s9d7f",LARGE({1;2;3;4;5;6;7;8;
9}*ISNUMBER(1*{"a";"a";"a";"8";"s";"9";"d";"7";"f"}),ROW(INDIRECT
("1:"&LEN(A2)))),1),0))
```

```
SUM(IFERROR({1;10;100;1000;10000;100000;1000000;
10000000;100000000}*MID("aaa8s9d7f",LARGE({0;0;0;4;0;6;0;8;
0},{1;2;3;4;5;6;7;8;9}),1),0))
```

```
SUM(IFERROR({1;10;100;1000;10000;100000;1000000;
10000000;100000000}*{"7";"9";"8";#VALUE!;#VALUE!;#VALUE!
;#VALUE!;#VALUE!;#VALUE!},0))
```

```
SUM(IFERROR({7;90;800;#VALUE!;#VALUE!;#VALUE!;#VALUE!
;#VALUE!;#VALUE!},0))
```

```
SUM({7;90;800;0;0;0;0;0;0})
```

VBA Topics

Partially Matching Words with a User-Defined Function

As you can see in column C of this figure, any word that columns A and B have in common is reported as a partial match, with the matching word in parentheses:

C1	▼	:	×	✓	f_x	=sameword(A1,B1)

	A	B	C
1	partial disk	this disk is nice	Partial match (disk)
2	RibbonX is hard	I don't like the new Ribbon	no match
3	Testing	Testing	Partial match (Testing)
4	Microsoft Corporation	IBM, Armonk	no match
5	Today is a nice day	He's usually nice	Partial match (nice)

We'll look more closely at this user-defined function (UDF), which is called SameWord. The logic is to form two arrays of words from each cell in columns A and B and compare them in a loop. If the UDF finds a match, it returns that word.

Here's the routine, which we'll examine one line at a time:

```
Function SameWord(rg1 As String, rg2 As String) As String
    wds1 = Split(rg1, " ")
    wds2 = Split(rg2, " ")
    For i = 0 To UBound(wds1)
        For j = 0 To UBound(wds2)
            If wds1(i) = wds2(j) Then
                SameWord = "Partial match (" & wds1(i) & ")"
                Exit Function
            End If
        Next
    Next
    SameWord = "no match"
End Function
```

The first line defines the function and specifies that there are two parameters, rg1 and rg2, which are both strings, and the function returns a string (indicated by the trailing As String):

```
Function SameWord(rg1 As String, rg2 As String) As String
```

The next two lines use the Split function, which makes an array of strings, using
```
                           wds1 = Split(rg1, " ")
```
the second parameter as a delimiter: `wds2 = Split(rg2, " ")`

That is, rg1 gets the text partial disk from A1, and Split makes an array consisting of the words partial and disk. The Split function gives zero-based results, so wds1(0) is partial, and wds1(1) is disk. You can cause a UDF to run in single-step

mode by putting a breakpoint on a line, as in the following example. With the
cursor on the line highlighted here, you press F9:

```
Function SameWord(rg1 As String, rg2 As String) As String
    wds1 = Split(rg1, " ")
    wds2 = Split(rg2, " ")
```

Then, if you go to the worksheet, select cell C1, press F2, and then press Enter
(to re-invoke the function), you see this:

```
Function SameWord(rg1 As String, rg2 As String) As String
    wds1 = Split(rg1, " ")
    wds2 = Split(rg2, " ")
    For i = 0 To UBound(wds1)
```

In the figure above, the highlighted line is the line that is about to be executed,
and the macro is paused. At this point, you can examine variables by selecting
View/Locals Window:

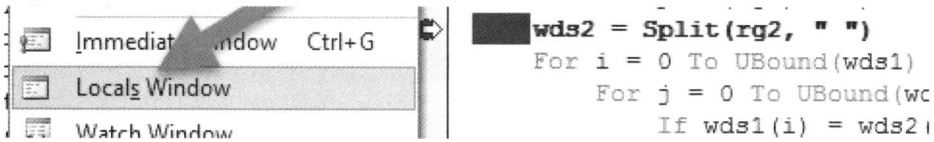

That window is then shown like this (you may have to resize it):

```
Function SameWord(rg1 As String, rg2 As String) As String
    wds1 = Split(rg1, " ")
    wds2 = Split(rg2, " ")
    For i = 0 To UBound(wds1)
        For j = 0 To UBound(wds2)
            If wds1(i) = wds2(j) Then
                SameWord = "Partial match (" & wds1(i) & ")"
                Exit Function
            End If
        Next
    Next
    SameWord = "no match"
```

Locals

VBAProject.Module1.SameWord

Expression	Value	Type
⊞ Module1		Module1/Module1
rg1	"partial disk"	String
rg2	"this disk is nice"	String
SameWord	""	String
⊞ wds1		Variant/String(0 to 1)
wds2	Empty	Variant/Empty

If you click the + by wds1, you see this:

wds2 is empty because the UDF hasn't executed that line yet.

Once you have values for wds1 and wds2, you have a nested loop that goes through all the possible pairs. The loop starts at 0, but how do you know what the upper limit is? The UBound function is made for this purpose. As shown here, you put a breakpoint after the inner loop and highlight UBound(wds2) and then press Shift+F9 to see the Quick Watch window, which in this case shows the value 3. That is, j goes from 0 to 3 because there are four words in wds2:

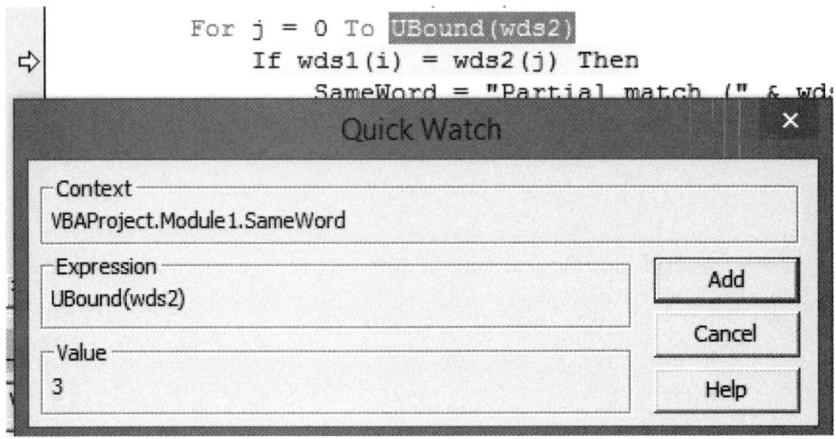

The test is shown here:

```
If wds1(i) = wds2(j) Then
    SameWord = "Partial match (" & wds1(i) & ")"
    Exit Function
End If
```

If any pair matches, the function name SameWord is set equal to the text "Partial match (", and the word is appended and a closing parenthesis is included. (wds1(i) is used here, but you could use wds2(i) just as well, since they're equal.) Because you now have the answer, you need to exit the function, or it will continue on and eventually get to the bottom and always return "no match":

```
                    Exit Function
                End If
            Next
        Next
        SameWord = "no match"
    End Function
```

You do want it to return "no match" if it hasn't exited the function when finding a match, so the code just falls through to the end of the nested loops.

Besides being useful, this UDF runs quite quickly!

Setting Up Many Check Boxes on a Worksheet

Say that you want to create a worksheet like this:

	A	B	C	D
1		☑ apple		TRUE
2		☐ banana		FALSE
3		☑ grape		TRUE
4		☐ watermelon		FALSE
5		☑ fig		TRUE
6		☐ date		FALSE
7		☑ cranberry		TRUE
8		☐ strawberry		FALSE
9		☑ raspberry		TRUE

Notice that the check boxes are linked to column D, and each check box fits nicely in the middle of its row. Setting this up might not be too difficult, but what if you had to set up 50 or 100 check boxes? This section describes a trick that makes doing so easy.

In a new sheet, you start by entering one check box by using the Developer tab:

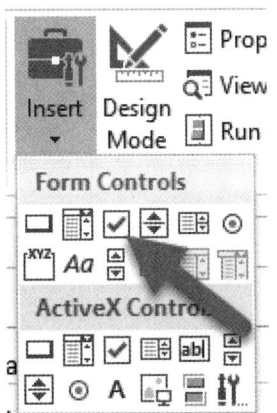

Select the Check Box tool and then click in the worksheet:

	B	C
	☐ Check Box 1	

Notice that the new check box is not quite centered in the vertical center of row

1; that's okay.

You want 10 of these check boxes, so hold the Ctrl key (to copy) and Shift (to keep the same vertical or horizontal orientation) and drag down:

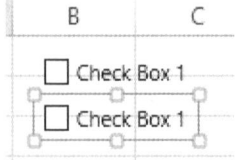

Now, Ctrl+click the first check box so both check boxes are selected (or you can press Ctrl+Shift+Spacebar to select all the objects on the sheet, assuming that one is already selected) and then drag down both check boxes and duplicate them, again by holding down Ctrl+Shift:

Notice that the check boxes are not evenly spaced at this point—but you'll fix that. Repeat the process you used before—pressing Ctrl+Shift+Spacebar to select all four and then Ctrl+Shift+drag to get eight check boxes in all:

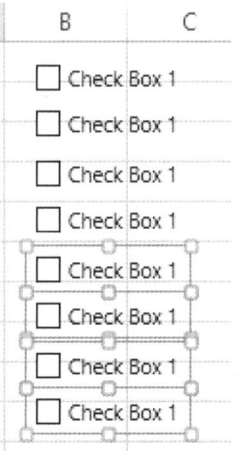

Now you need two more, so you click on a cell to deselect all check boxes and then Ctrl+click on one and Ctrl+click on another so two are selected. Then you do one last Ctrl+Shift+drag, to get this:

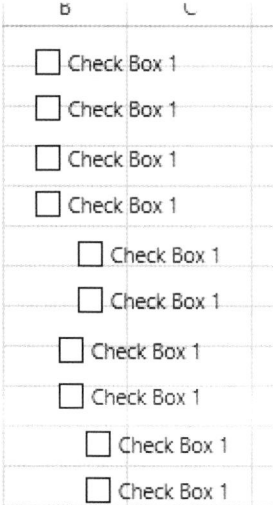

By the way, if your check boxes are aligned raggedly, like this:

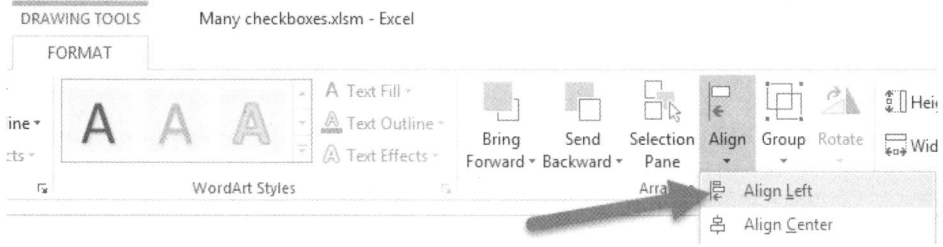

you can select them all and then from the contextual Format tab, select Align Left:

But notice that these check boxes go into row 12, and you want them in row 10.

You can change the row height of the whole worksheet so that the bottom check box fits in row 10:

Ouch! You only wanted the row height to change; you didn't want the check boxes to move! So to undo this, you Ctrl+click one check box, press Ctrl+-Shift+Spacebar to select them all, and you get this right-click menu:

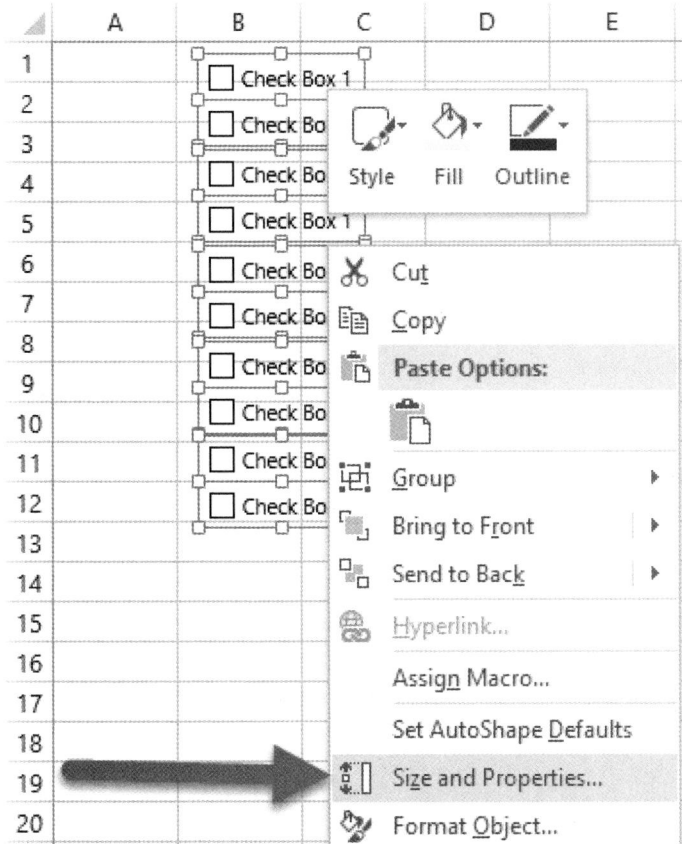

Select the Size and Properties item. In Excel 2013, you now see the Format Shape flyout. (In earlier Excel versions, you see a comparable dialog.) In this fly-out, open the Properties section, and you see the Don't Move or Size with Cells item, which you should select:

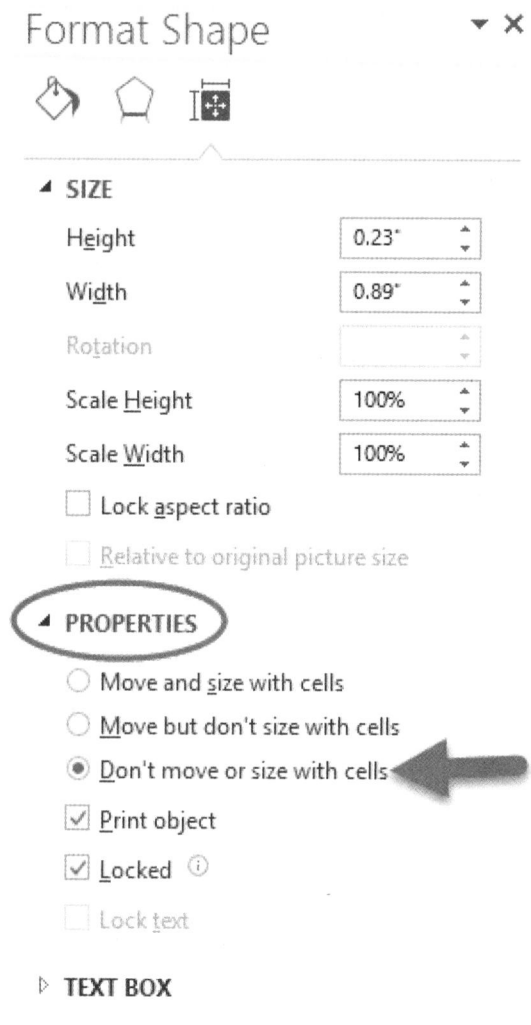

Since you're giving this property to the selection, which is all the check boxes, you can now try to make the row heights bigger again:

Well, this is better because they didn't move, but now the check boxes are too close together. Here comes some more magic: Ctrl+click the bottom check box only and drag it down to row 10. As you do this, hold down the Shift key, not the Ctrl key, to keep this check box aligned with the others. Also, if the top check box isn't centered in row 1, drag that to put it in the center:

Ctrl+Shift+Spacebar to once again select all the check boxes and then select the Format tab again, where you'll find a great feature, Distribute Vertically:

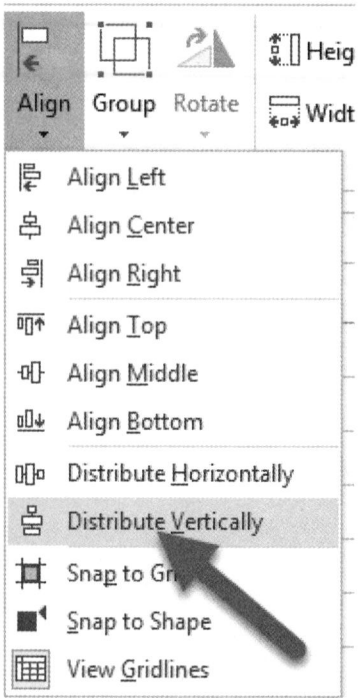

When you select Distribute Vertically, look what happens:

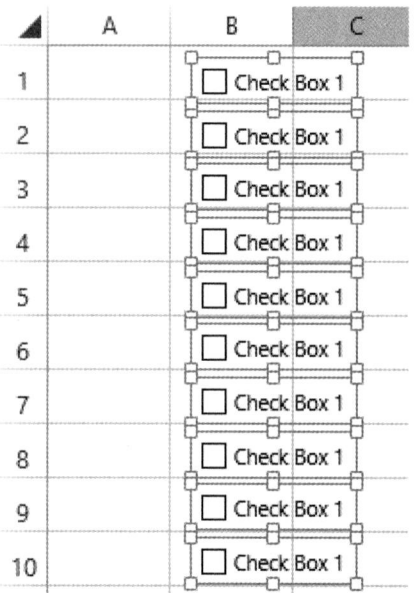

Perfect! Okay, now you need to change the descriptions and assign the check boxes to cells. You can record a macro to handle the first one. Then you can look at the VBA code that's created and edit it to handle all the check boxes. To get going, click the top check box and then in the Developer tab, click Record Macro:

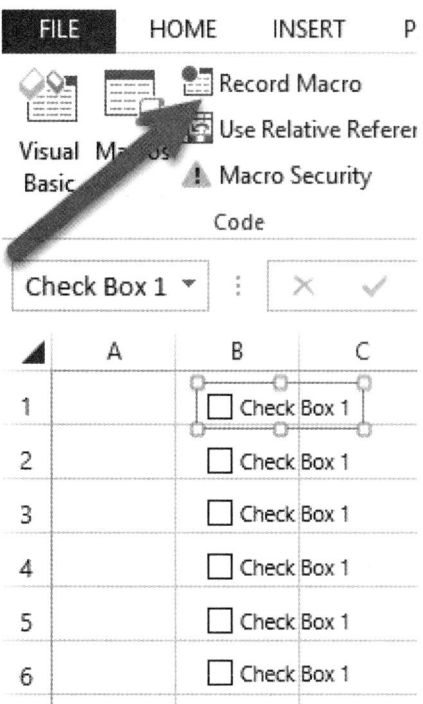

After you click Record Macro, right-click the first check box, select Format Control, and then assign the check box to cell D1, which you can do by clicking inside the Cell Link box and then clicking cell D1 or by typing it in as shown here:

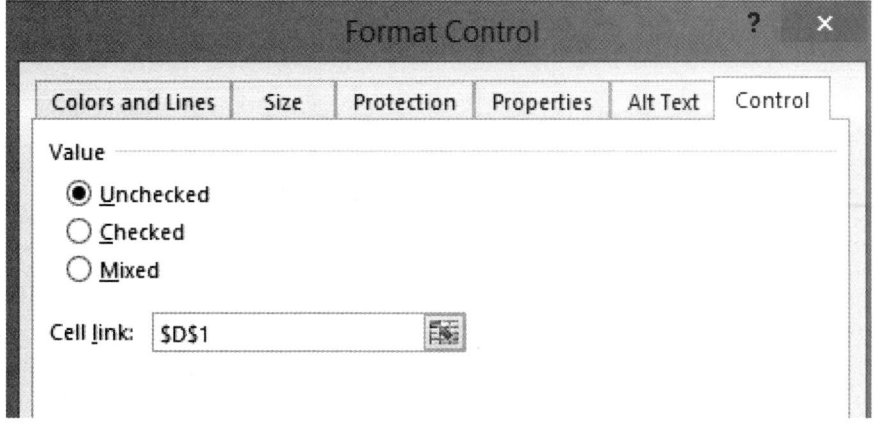

Then type the word apple and press the esc key. Finally, click Stop Recording on the Developer tab (where it said Record Macro before).

The macro's VBA code looks something like this:

```
Sub Macro1()
'
' Macro1 Macro
'


    ActiveSheet.Shapes.Range(Array("Check Box 1")).Select
    With Selection
        .Value = xlOn
        .LinkedCell = "$D$1"
        .Display3DShading = False
    End With
    Selection.Characters.Text = "apple"
End Sub
```

The only lines of this macro that you're interested in are the LinkedCell property and the Selection.Characters.Text statement. If you refer to the initial screenshot in this section, you'll see all the fruit names in the check boxes. You can type them into column F, temporarily, and the macro will become fairly trivial. Here's what you start with:

B	C	D	E	F	G
☑ apple		TRUE		apple	
☐ Check Box 1				banana	
☐ Check Box 1				grape	
☐ Check Box 1				watermelon	
☐ Check Box 1				fig	
☐ Check Box 1				date	
☐ Check Box 1				cranberry	
☐ Check Box 1				strawberry	
☐ Check Box 1				raspberry	
☐ Check Box 1				blueberry	

Then you can easily modify the macro that was recorded:

```
Sub Assigner()
    For i = 1 To 10
        ActiveSheet.CheckBoxes(i).LinkedCell = Cells(i, 4).Address
        ActiveSheet.CheckBoxes(i).Characters.Text = Cells(i, 6).Value
    Next
End Sub
```

Notice a few things:

- You don't have to select anything.

- Since the recorded macro shows that the LinkedCell property is expecting an A1-type address, you use Cells(i, 4).Address, which, when i is 1, is Cells(1, 4).Address, which is $D$1.

- The text for the characters sits in column F (or Cells(i, 6).Value). This could also be written as ActiveSheet.Checkboxes(i).Caption = Cells(i, 6).Value (without .Characters.).

Here's the result:

B	C	D	E	F	G
☑ apple		TRUE		apple	
☐ banana				banana	
☐ grape				grape	
☐ watermelon				watermelon	
☐ fig				fig	
☐ date				date	
☐ cranberry				cranberry	
☐ strawberry				strawberry	
☐ raspberry				raspberry	
☐ blueberry				blueberry	

You can now clear column F and test the check boxes by clicking them.

Narrowing Down What Caused a Crash

Sometimes Excel simply gives a message along the lines of "Excel has stopped working. We are sorry for any inconvenience."

When you get such a message, you might press Ctrl+Alt+Delete and open the workbook again (hopefully having saved whatever work you had done!), wanting to step through the code to find the offending statement. When you single-step through the code, all may work fine, but when you run it at full speed, once again it may crash. How can you find the offending statement?

You can write a simple line of code between each line of code that could be the culprit. So the VBA code may originally look something like this:

```
Sub UICreation()
Dim x As String
    On Error Resume Next
    x = Sheets("Scenario").Name
    If Err.Number <> 0 Then
        MsgBox "Current workbook needs to have a Scenario sheet!", vbCritical
        Exit Sub
    End If
    ActiveWorkbook.Unprotect WorkbookPassword
    Err.Clear
    ActiveWorkbook.Unprotect SheetPassword
    If Err.Number <> 0 Then
        MsgBox "Workbook cannot be unprotected by the macro.", vbCritical
        Exit Sub
    End If
    Application.OnTime Now, "More"
    ThisWorkbook.Sheets("FastPricer").Copy Before:=ActiveWorkbook.Sheets(1)
End Sub
```

This procedure, in fact, does not crash, but it illustrates what you can do if you find that code crashes when run at full speed but not when you step through it.

You change the above code to this, with inserted statements Bug 1, Bug 2, etc.:

```
Sub UICreation()
Dim x As String
    On Error Resume Next
    Bug 1
    x = Sheets("Scenario").Name
    Bug 2
    If Err.Number <> 0 Then
        MsgBox "Current workbook needs to have a Scenario sheet!", vbCritical
        Exit Sub
    End If
    Bug 3
    ActiveWorkbook.Unprotect WorkbookPassword
    Err.Clear
    Bug 4
    ActiveWorkbook.Unprotect SheetPassword
    If Err.Number <> 0 Then
        MsgBox "Workbook cannot be unprotected by the macro.", vbCritical
        Exit Sub
    End If
    Bug 5
    Application.OnTime Now, "More"
    Bug 6
    ThisWorkbook.Sheets("FastPricer").Copy Before:=ActiveWorkbook.Sheets(1)
End Sub
```

Here's the bug procedure:

```
Sub Bug(num As Integer)
    SaveSetting "EOTB2", "EOTB2", "EOTB2", num
End Sub
```

This procedure saves a value in the registry. The syntax for SaveSetting is:

```
savesetting |
```

SaveSetting(**AppName As String**, Section As String, Key As String, Setting As String)

For the first three parameters, say that you use EOTB2 (for Excel Outside the Box 2)—a random selection. You could instead use SaveSetting "X","X","X",num. If you use this a lot, you can take advantage of the three levels AppName, Section, and Key. That way, if you have many sections in the AppName, you can clean up the registry for all your settings by using the simple DeleteSetting "EOTB2" (or whatever you set for AppName), and all the sections and keys will also be deleted.

Now you run the procedure at full speed, and it crashes. So you restart Excel, get to the VBE, open the Immediate window (by pressing Ctrl+G), and type this:

? GetSetting("EOTB2","EOTB2","EOTB2")

If this procedure returns 4, for example, then it crashed sometime after Bug 4. It's unlikely that the If/End If section was the culprit; more likely it was ActiveWorkbook.Unprotect SheetPassword. (Remember that this is just an example, not what has actually happened.)

If your initial run of Bug 1, Bug 2, etc. shows that the procedure crashed in a large section of code after Bug x, you can insert more bug calls to narrow it down further. You sort of do a binary search in a long procedure to find the culprit.

Filling a List Box with Months

Say that you want to create a user form with a list box containing months and then fill it upon initialization of the form, sort of like this:

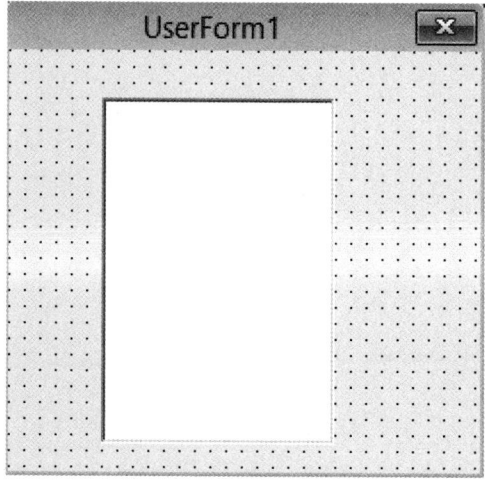

```
Private Sub UserForm_Initialize()
    For i = 1 To 12
        Me.ListBox1.AddItem Sheet1.Cells(i, 4).Value
    Next
End Sub
```

In this case, the worksheet Sheet1 contains:

D
January
February
March
April
May
June
July
August
September
October
November
December

And the form looks like this:

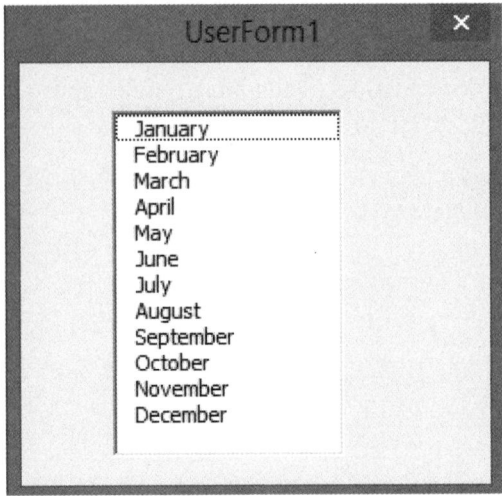

This works well, but note that you do have to have a worksheet that contains the months. One way to handle this is to manually type the month names into a worksheet (or get them in by typing January and using the fill handle for 12 rows to get the rest)

Another way to do the same thing, without using any VBA (but still needing a worksheet containing the months), is to use RowSource to point to the range. In the design of the user form, you click the list box to activate it and then enter the RowSource parameter:

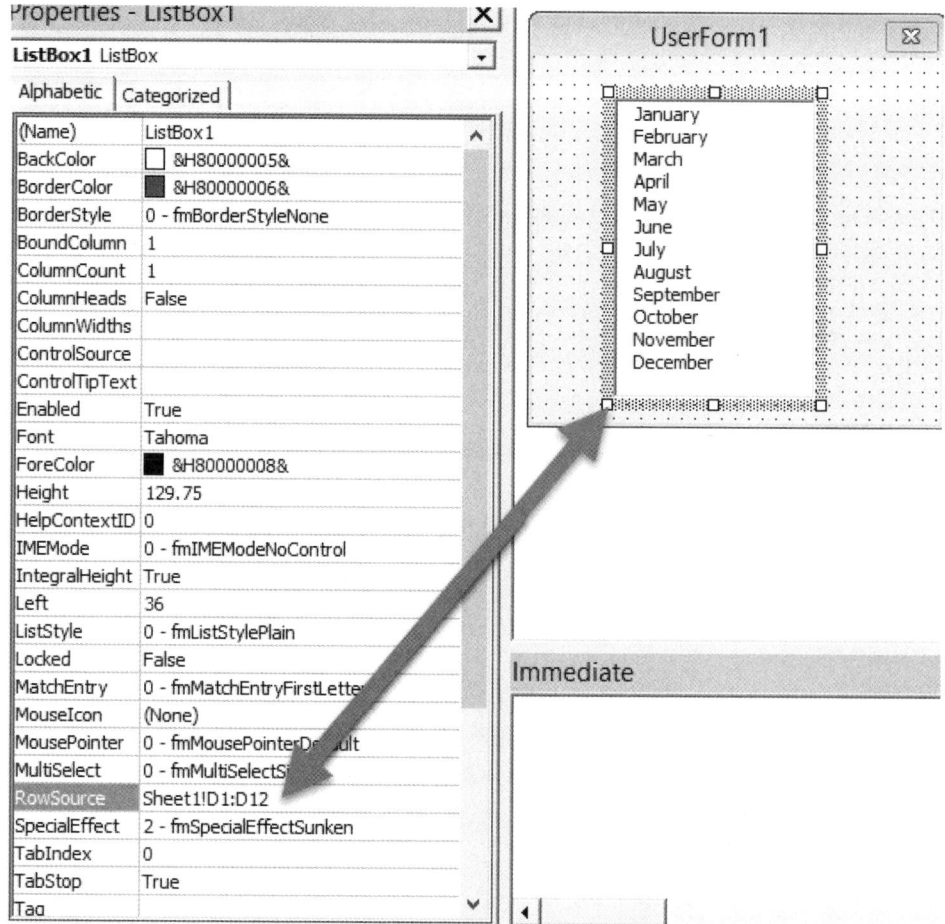

As soon as you do that, the list is filled in, even in design mode.

Here's one way you can fill a worksheet with the months by using VBA:

```
Private Sub UserForm_Initialize()
    For i = 0 To 11
        Me.ListBox1.AddItem Array("January", "February", "March", "April", "May", "June", _
        "July", "August", "September", "October", "November", "December")(i)
    Next
End Sub
```

Notice that the loop goes from 0 to 11 since this kind of array is zero-based.

Actually, I think that this method is painful because you have to type in each month name—even though you don't need to take up room in a worksheet!

Here's another alternative:

```
Private Sub UserForm_Initialize()
    For i = 1 To 12
        Me.ListBox1.AddItem Format(DateValue(i & "/1/2000")
    Next
End Sub
```

This is an interesting solution: You don't have to type any month names. The first
time through the loop, i is 1, the field inside DateValue is 1/1/2000 (any other
year would work as well), and you format this date as the full month name.

But the best approach doesn't use a loop at all, since these dates already exist
in the custom lists. In File/Options/Advanced, near the bottom, you see the Edit
Custom Lists button:

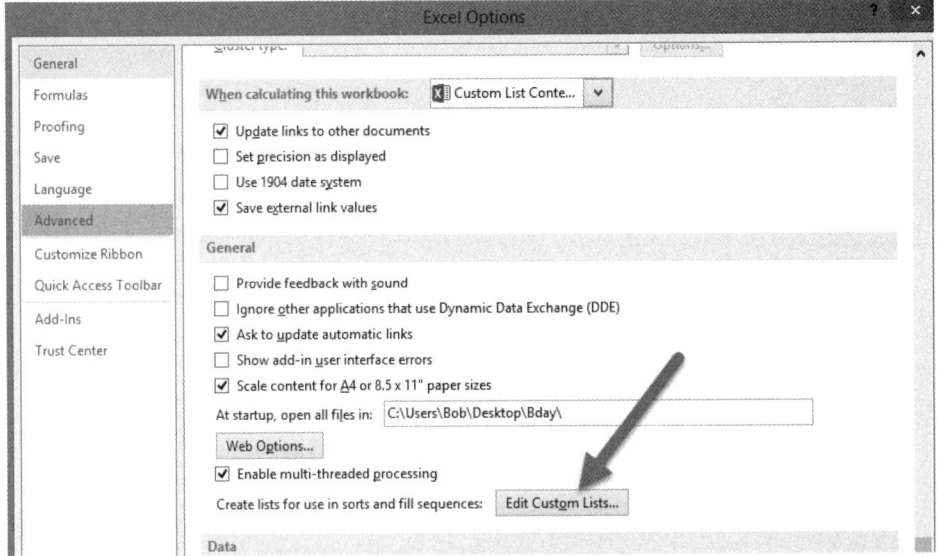

When you click the Edit Custom Lists button, you see the built-in and custom
lists:

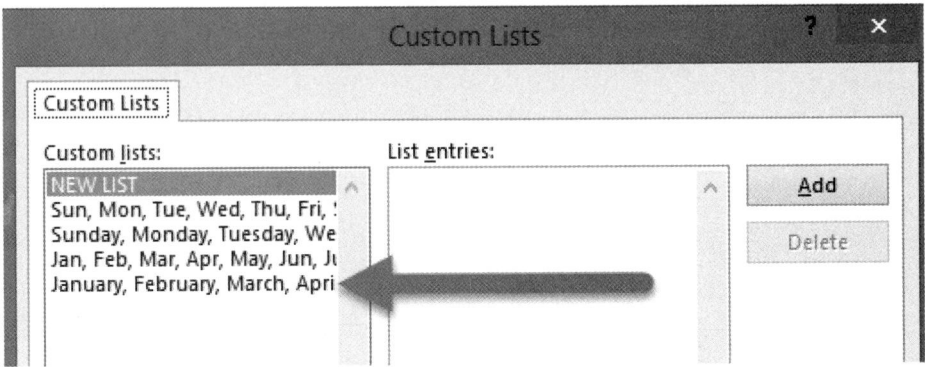

Notice that the fourth custom list is the one you're looking for, and it is available
via VBA. Here's the Initialize procedure:

```
Private Sub UserForm_Initialize()
    Me.ListBox1.List = Application.GetCustomListContents(4)
End Sub
```

I think this method is the best and most versatile: It gives you access to any of the custom lists.

Filtering by Data in a Text Box

Imagine that you're working with this worksheet:

◢	A
1	type ▼
2	one
3	two
4	one
5	one
6	three
7	three
8	four
9	three
10	one
11	one
12	two
13	four
14	

and this text box:

C	D	E	F

When you enter the text one in the text box and click outside the text box, you see:

◢	A	B	C	D	E	F
1	type					
2	one					
4	one			one		
5	one					
10	one					
11	one					
14						

and of course, if you enter two, you see:

◢	A	B	C	D	E	F
1	type					
3	two					
12	two			two		
14						
15						
16						
17						

You can implement this text box fairly easily with a one-line macro in the Selection Change event of the sheet. Right-click the sheet tab, select View Code, and enter this:

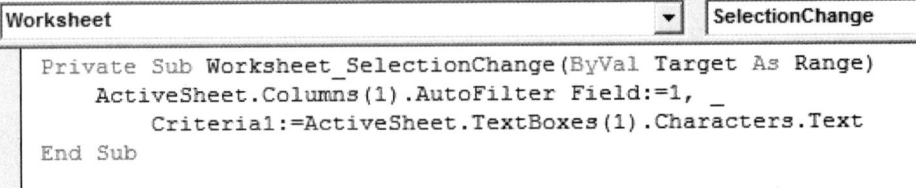

```
Worksheet                                              ▼    SelectionChange

Private Sub Worksheet_SelectionChange(ByVal Target As Range)
    ActiveSheet.Columns(1).AutoFilter Field:=1, _
        Criteria1:=ActiveSheet.TextBoxes(1).Characters.Text
End Sub
```

As soon as you click a cell other than the last one clicked to invoke Selection-Change, the macro runs; it filters the sheet based on the text in the text box.

Creating a Summary Chart with a Single Click

The idea and technique for this trick come from a friend, Joe Sorrenti. Look at this figure:

	A	B	C	D	E	F	G	
1	Sales (in thousands)							
2								
3	2000 Jan		Feb	Mar	Apr	May	Jun	Ju
4	Apples	1,687	2,480	1,120	1,724	2,078	1,656	
5	Oranges	1,910	1,782	3,003	2,697	1,500	1,236	
6	Peaches	1,856	1,705	2,447	2,147	1,882	1,600	
7	Pears	2,150	1,776	1,955	2,386	1,319	1,883	
8	Total	7,603	7,743	8,525	8,954	6,779	6,375	
9								
10	2001 Jan		Feb	Mar	Apr	May	Jun	Ju
11	Apples	2,951	2,683	2,385	1,560	1,261	2,087	
12	Oranges	685	2,006	2,894	1,697	2,250	1,990	
13	Peaches	2,388	2,060	2,256	1,842	2,110	3,241	
14	Pears	1,725	2,142	2,375	2,470	2,755	1,834	
15	Total	7,749	8,891	9,910	7,569	8,376	9,152	
16								
17	2002 Jan		Feb	Mar	Apr	May	Jun	Ju
18	Apples	1,885	2,867	1,843	2,114	1,568	1,816	
19	Oranges	2,194	1,657	2,346	1,911	2,197	1,845	
20	Peaches	1,131	2,366	1,844	1,694	1,746	3,049	
21	Pears	1,522	1,711	2,731	2,458	1,758	1,525	
22	Total	6,732	8,601	8,764	8,177	7,269	8,235	

◄ ► | NY | NJ | PA | CT | **Total** ... ⊕ ⋮ ◄▯

You're looking at the Total tab, where each formula is a sum from NY through CT. (Actually, there are two invisible tabs: First, which is before the first tab, and Last, which is before the Total tab. Each cell contains the same relative formula. For example, here's the one in cell B4: =SUM(First:Last!B4).

Here's what happens when you click on cell B4 in the Total tab:

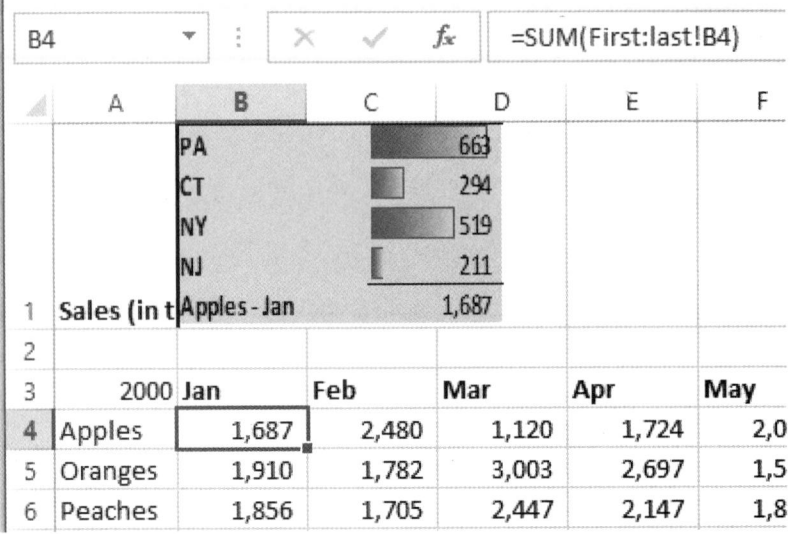

| | B4 | | ⋮ | ✕ | ✓ | *fx* | =SUM(First:last!B4) |

⟋	A	B	C	D	E	F
		PA			663		
		CT			294		
		NY			519		
		NJ			211		
1	Sales (in t	Apples - Jan			1,687		
2						
3	2000	Jan	Feb	Mar	Apr	May
4	Apples	1,687	2,480	1,120	1,724	2,0
5	Oranges	1,910	1,782	3,003	2,697	1,5
6	Peaches	1,856	1,705	2,447	2,147	1,8

And here's what you see when you click cell F7:

| | F7 | | ⋮ | ✕ | ✓ | *fx* | =SUM(First:last!F7) |

⟋	A	B	C	D	E	F	G	H
1	Sales (in thousands)					PA		98
						CT		300
2						NY		707
3	2000	Jan	Feb	Mar	Apr	NJ		214
4	Apples	1,687	2,480	1,120	1,724	Pears - May		1,319 286
5	Oranges	1,910	1,782	3,003	2,697	1,500	1,236	1,030
6	Peaches	1,856	1,705	2,447	2,147	1,882	1,600	2,252
7	Pears	2,150	1,776	1,955	2,386	1,319	1,883	1,868
8	Total	7,603	7,743	8,525	8,954	6,779	6,375	6,43(

Pretty cool! The following figures show each tab's F7 (shown in the order of the little embedded popup chart: PA, CT, NY, NJ):

| F7 | | ▼ | ⋮ | ✕ | ✓ | *fx* | 98 | |

◢	A	B	C	D	E	F	
1	Sales (in thousands)						
2							
3	2000	Jan	Feb	Mar	Apr	May	Ju
4	Apples	663	630	170	835	658	
5	Oranges	152	889	779	984	823	
6	Peaches	209	844	598	665	5	
7	Pears	165	290	923	946	98	
8	Total	1,189	2,653	2,470	3,430	1,584	

| F7 | | ▼ | ⋮ | ✕ | ✓ | *fx* | 300 | |

◢	A	B	C	D	E	F	
1	Sales (in thousands)						
2							
3	2000	Jan	Feb	Mar	Apr	May	Jı
4	Apples	294	945	304	496	527	
5	Oranges	791	8	733	137	488	
6	Peaches	997	345	259	810	986	
7	Pears	543	802	275	395	300	
8	Total	2,625	2,100	1,571	1,838	2,301	

| F7 | | ▼ | ⋮ | ✕ | ✓ | *fx* | 707 | |

◢	A	B	C	D	E	F	
1	Sales (in thousands)						
2							
3	2000	Jan	Feb	Mar	Apr	May	J
4	Apples	519	150	630	95	710	
5	Oranges	278	556	868	894	104	
6	Peaches	198	494	612	339	385	
7	Pears	787	23	433	900	707	
8	Total	1,782	1,223	2,543	2,228	1,906	

F7	▼	⋮	×	✓	f_x	214

◢	A	B	C	D	E	F
1	Sales (in thousands)					
2						
3	2000	Jan	Feb	Mar	Apr	May	J
4	Apples	211	755	16	298	183
5	Oranges	689	329	623	682	85
6	Peaches	452	22	978	333	506
7	Pears	655	661	324	145	214
8	Total	2,007	1,767	1,941	1,458	988

You can clearly see each number in the chart, even though the Total tab shows only the total. Okay, how do you do this? With a little bit of VBA and a hidden picture.

In the Total tab, way out in range IT107:IX112, you see this—the picture that appears when you click cell F7:

IS107	▼	⋮	×	✓	f_x	

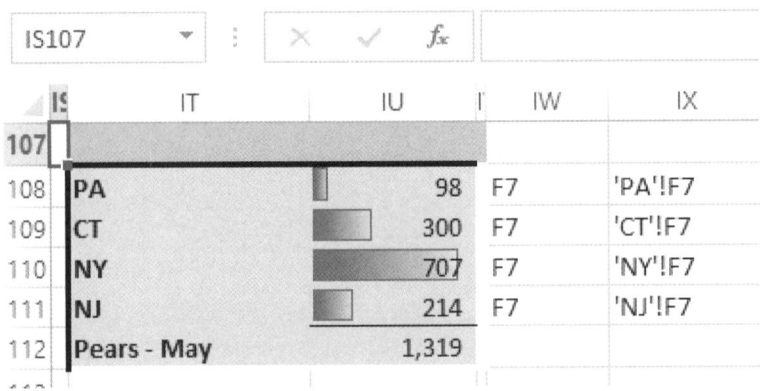

◢	IS	IT	IU	I'	IW	IX
107						
108	PA		98	F7		'PA'!F7
109	CT		300	F7		'CT'!F7
110	NY		707	F7		'NY'!F7
111	NJ		214	F7		'NJ'!F7
112	Pears - May		1,319			

Here are the underlying formulas:

◢	IS	IT	IU	IV	IW	IX
107						
108	PA		=INDIRECT(IX108)	F7		="'" &IT108 & "'!"&IW108
109	CT		=INDIRECT(IX109)	F7		="'" &IT109 & "'!"&IW109
110	NY		=INDIRECT(IX110)	F7		="'" &IT110 & "'!"&IW110
111	NJ		=INDIRECT(IX111)	F7		="'" &IT111 & "'!"&IW111
112	=INDEX(A:A,ROW(INDIRECT(IW108)))&"	=SUM(IU108:IU111)				

Before we examine these formulas in detail, let's take a little look at the VBA that updates just IW108:IW111, also called Range("AddressCells"). Also, you can see Shapes("myPopup") here:

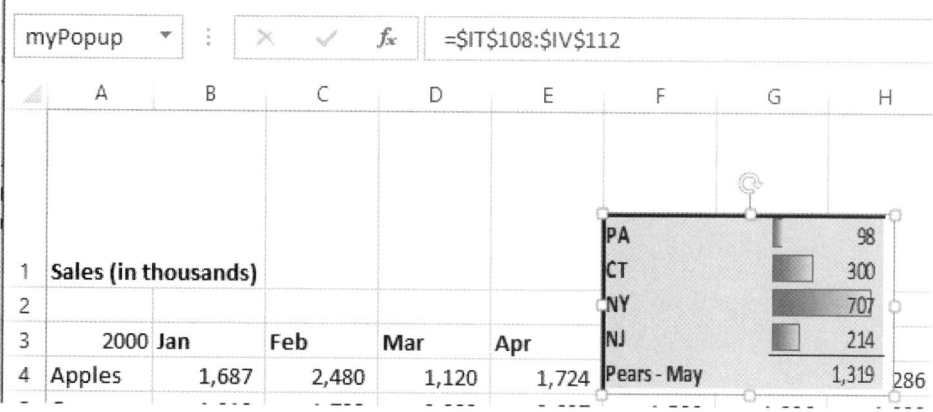

You create this shape by using the Camera tool. (For a refresher on how to access the Camera tool, see the section "Truncating Text and Showing an Ellipsis (…)," on page 21.) You select cells IT108 through IU112 and then use the Camera tool. Then you click anywhere in the document, and you see this:

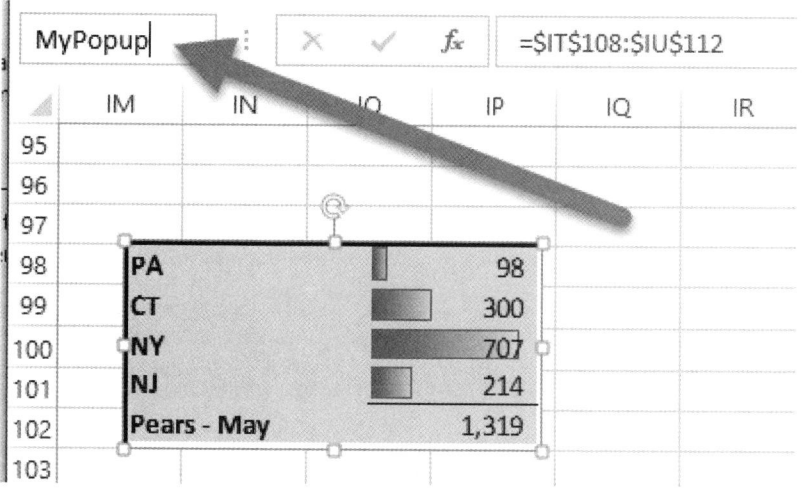

The Name box shows Picture 2. You can click there and type myPopup:

You can then make this box invisible by clicking Home/Find & Select/Selection Pane:

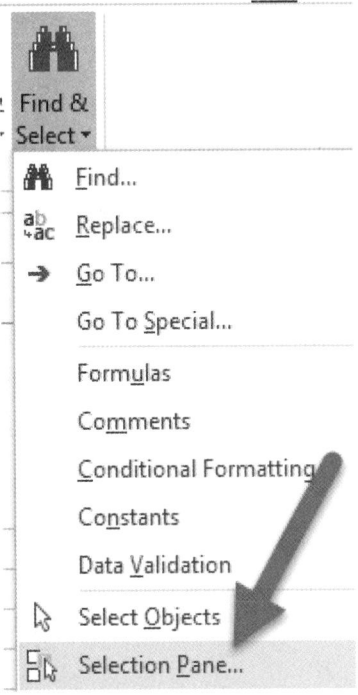

Then, when you click the eye icon, the image disappears, and in Excel 2013 you see this:

The VBA runs on a SelectionChange event. If the selection contains a formula and only one cell is selected, the macro fills the range AddressCells and calculates. This calculation fills all the numbers needed in the range used in the popup.

IX108 contains the formula:

="""" &IT108 & "'!"&IW108

IT108 contains the constant "PA", so this is ="'PA'!"&IW108, but it is all as a string, so cell IU108 uses the INDIRECT function, which turns it into a range and then picks up the 98 in the PA sheet.

Cell IT112 contains the formula:

=INDEX(A:A,ROW(INDIRECT(IW108)))&" - "&INDEX(3:3,,COLUMN(IN-DIRECT(IW108)))

which picks up the labels from column A and row 3, yielding in this case Pears –
May.

The next part of the macro places the popup and makes it visible. In the case of
F7, Target.Offset(-2,0).Top is 122, and the popup's height is 78, so dbltop is 44,
and the Left property is set to the Target's left, so it lines up correctly. Note that
you use MAX(0,…) to avoid a possible error, especially if row 1 is not set to be
so tall.

If there's no formula or if you select more than one cell, the macro makes the
popup invisible:

```
Private Sub Worksheet_SelectionChange(ByVal Target As Range
   Dim strAddress As String
   Dim shpPopup As Shape
   Dim dblTop As Double

   Set shpPopup = Me.Shapes("myPopup")
   On Error Resume Next
   If Target.Cells(1).HasFormula And Selection.Cells.Count =
      strAddress = Target.Cells(1).Address(False, False)
      Me.Range("AddressCells").Value = strAddress
      Me.Calculate
      dblTop = Application.Max(0, Target.Offset(-2, 0).Top -
      With shpPopup
         .Top = dblTop
         .Left = Target.Left
         .Visible = True
```

Copying Modules or User Forms from One Project to Another

Did you know that if you have a user form in one project, you can copy it by dragging it from the Project window of one project to another? For example, here you can click on UserForm1 from Book1 and drag it into Book2 (notice the + near the cursor):

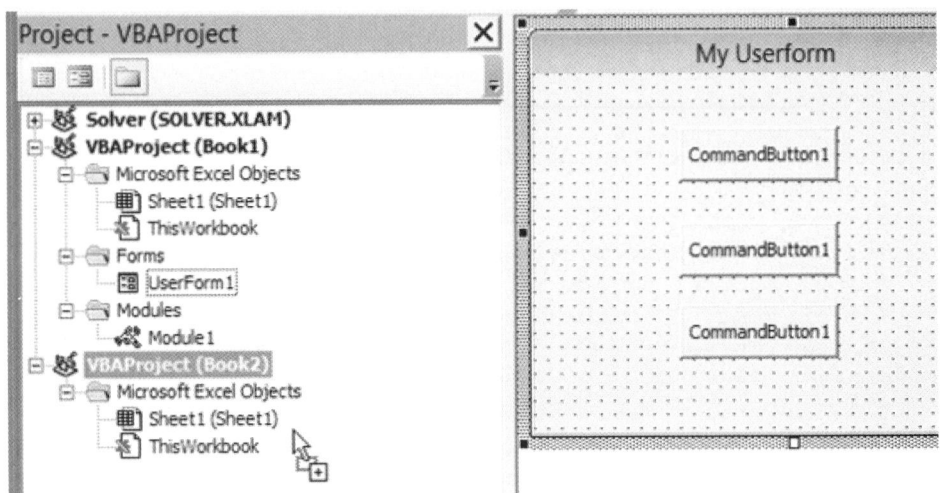

When you let go of the mouse, you see this:

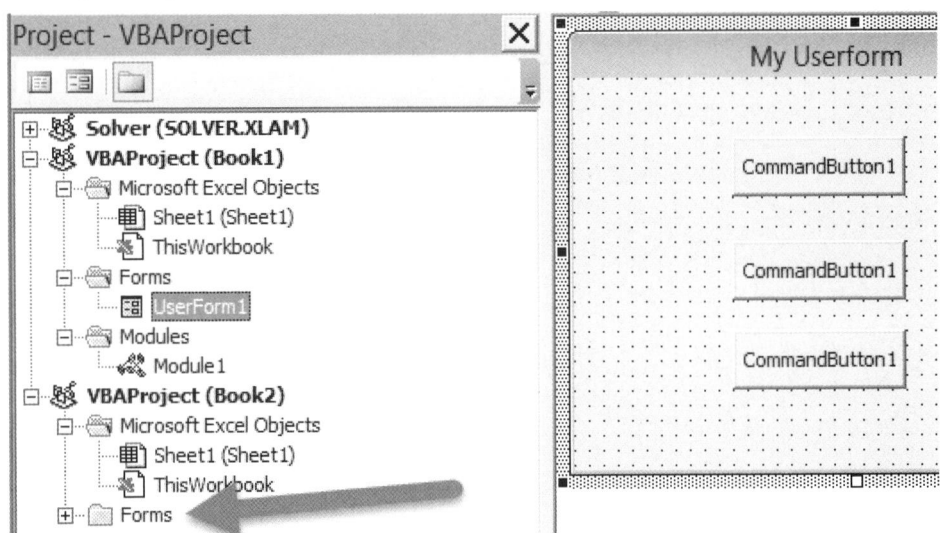

Notice the Forms folder in Book2? Inside it is a copy of the user form:

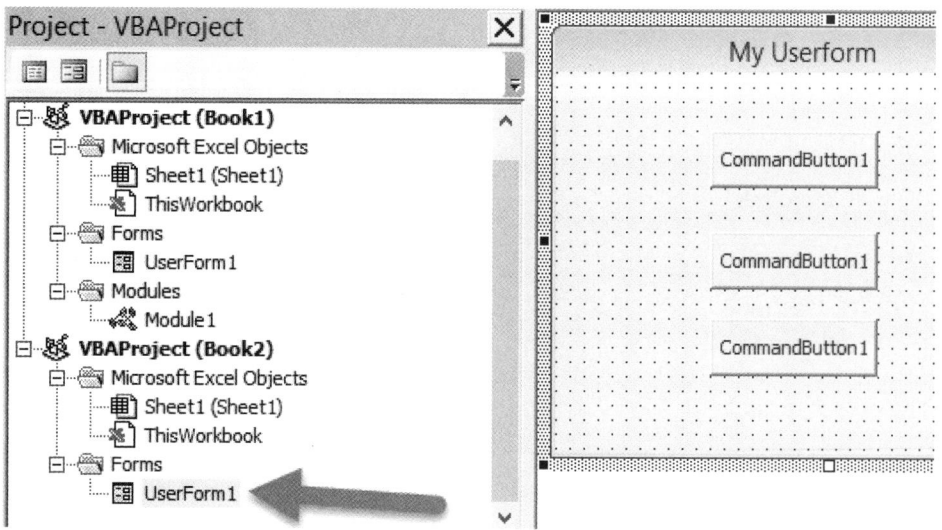

Keep in mind that you can do this with modules as well as with user forms!

Using the Locals Window in VBA

Most VBA programmers think of the Locals window as a good place to report on the contents of variables, among other things. But did you know the variables here are not read-only? Have a look! Here's a very simple procedure, in which the object variable MyVar is set to range B2; you can see from the worksheet in the background that this range contains 3. When you click Locals Window:

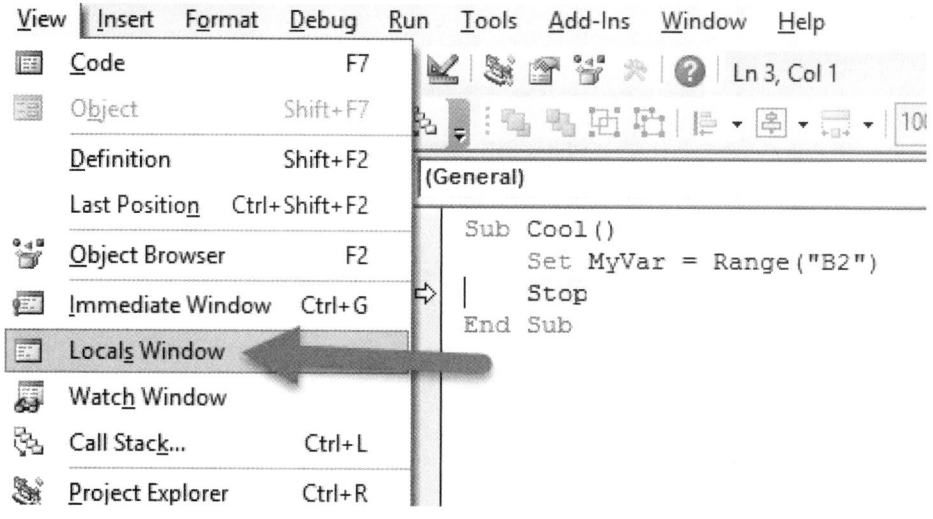

you see this:

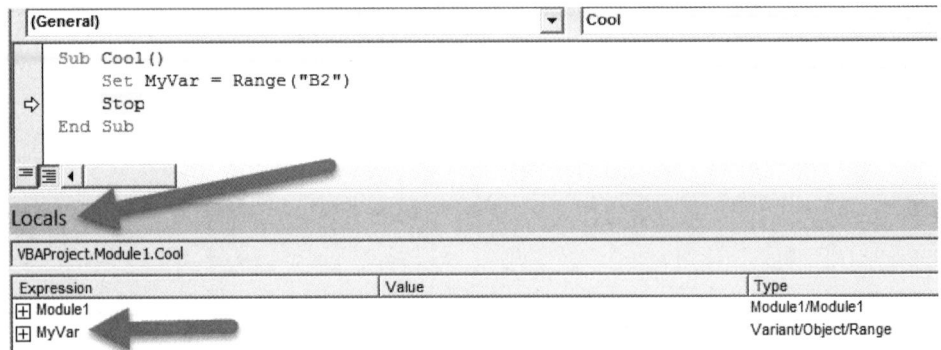

The object variable MyVar is shown as being expandable, since it's a Range object. When you click the + to the left and scroll down to the Value property, you see this:

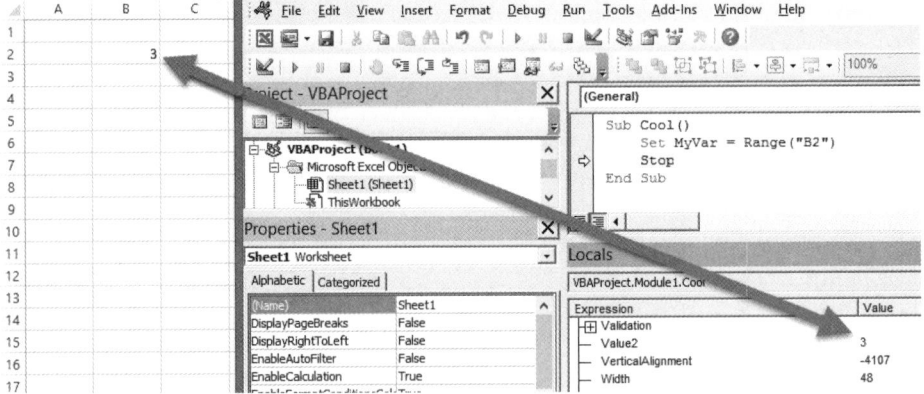

Obviously, this tells you that the value (shown as Value2 here) is 3. What's really cool, though, is that you can double-click on that 3 in the Locals window and change it to any value you want. For example, when you change it to 88 and press Enter, you see it change in the worksheet in the background:

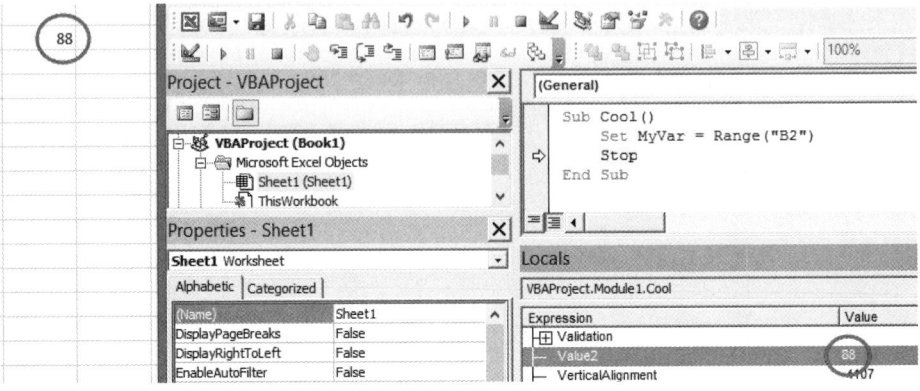

In this next example, ap is an object variable set equal to Application (Excel). When you reach End Sub, ScreenUpdating is True, but you can change it to False in the Locals window:

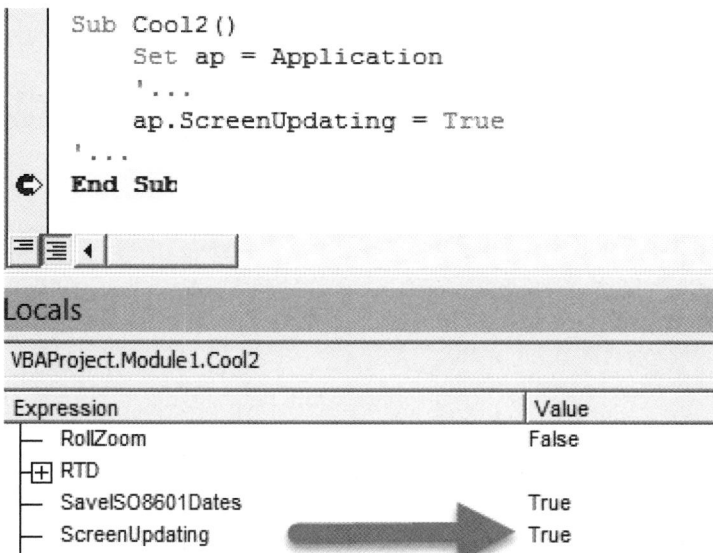

```
Sub Cool2()
    Set ap = Application
    '...
    ap.ScreenUpdating = True
'...
End Sub
```

Locals

VBAProject.Module1.Cool2

Expression	Value
— RollZoom	False
⊞ RTD	
— SaveISO8601Dates	True
— ScreenUpdating	True

You can also do this with normal variables, not just object variables. Here you see that the value of a is 5, but you can change it to 12 before MsgBox is executed:

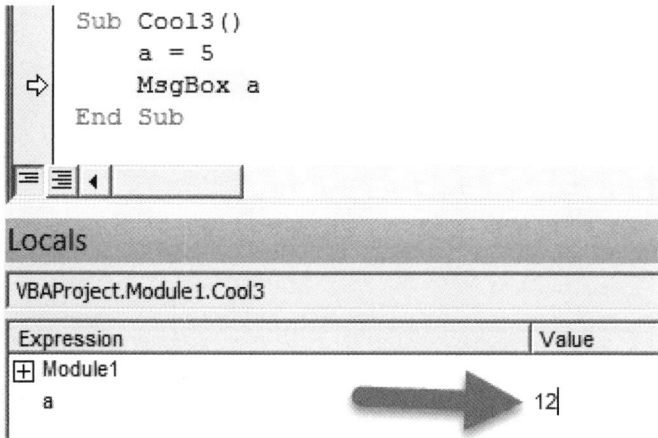

```
Sub Cool3()
    a = 5
    MsgBox a
End Sub
```

Locals

VBAProject.Module1.Cool3

Expression	Value
⊞ Module1	
a	12

If you now press F5, you see this:

Miscellaneous Topics

Creating a Gantt Chart from Many Sources (on Steroids!)

Say that you have three worksheets and a chart of the data, as shown here:

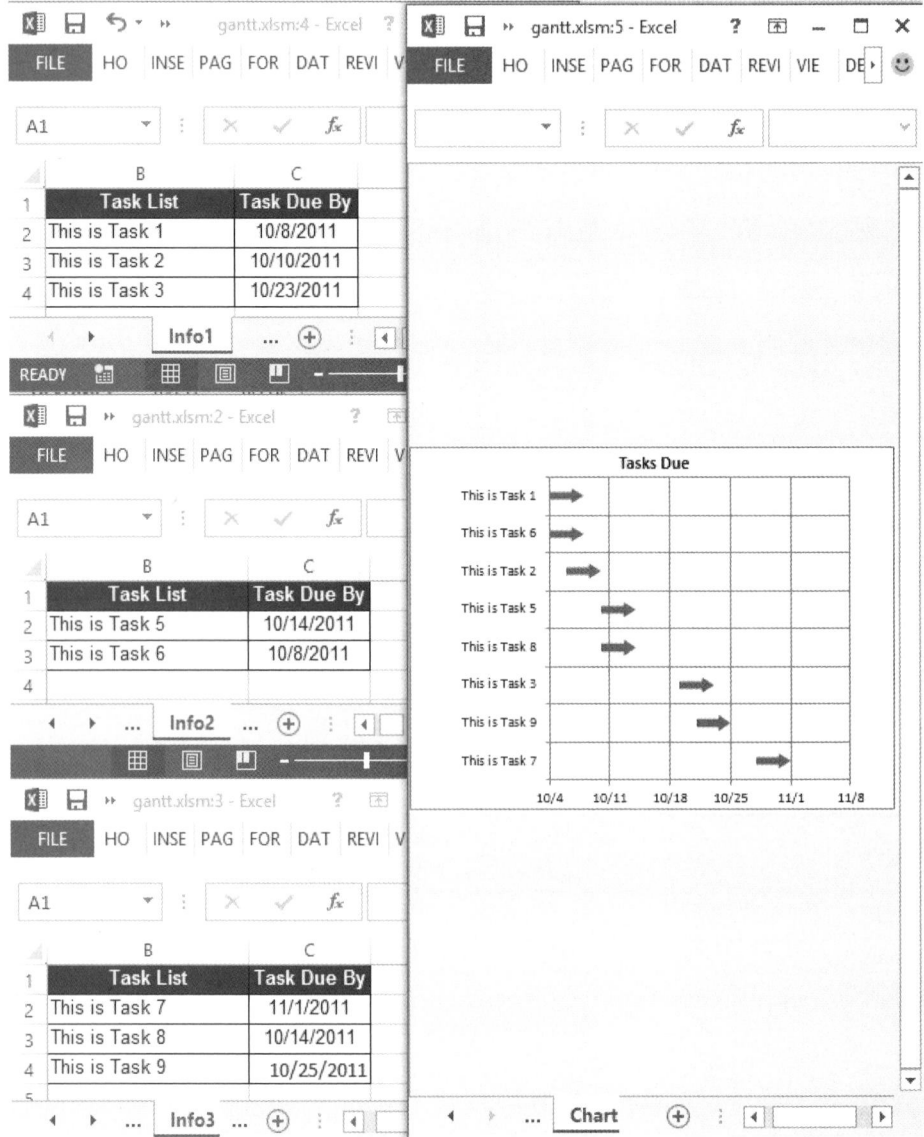

You can tell from the titles that this is one workbook split into four windows. The data in the chart is gathered from the first three sheets. What makes this special is that you can change data on any sheet by typing new data, deleting a row, cutting/pasting, etc., and the chart will reflect the changes effortlessly—and all with formulas. Actually, one teeny macro runs when the chart sheet is activated to change the scale on the Value axis by setting the axis to the earliest date in all the sheets.

The following shows what happens when you delete Task 2, add Task 6.5 to Info2 by inserting it before row 2, and add Task 10 to Info3:

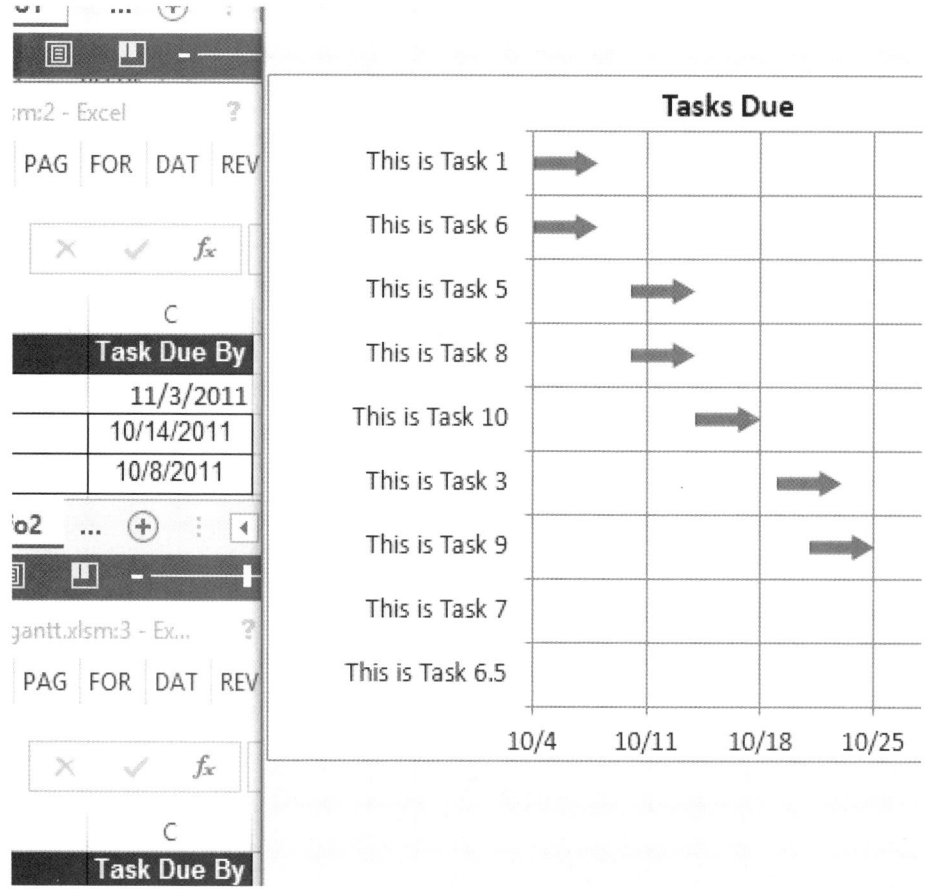

Notice that in the updated chart, the arrows end on the Task Due dates.

The secret? Well, there's some pretty involved stuff on a hidden sheet, which we will examine shortly. But first, look at the two SERIES formulas in the chart:

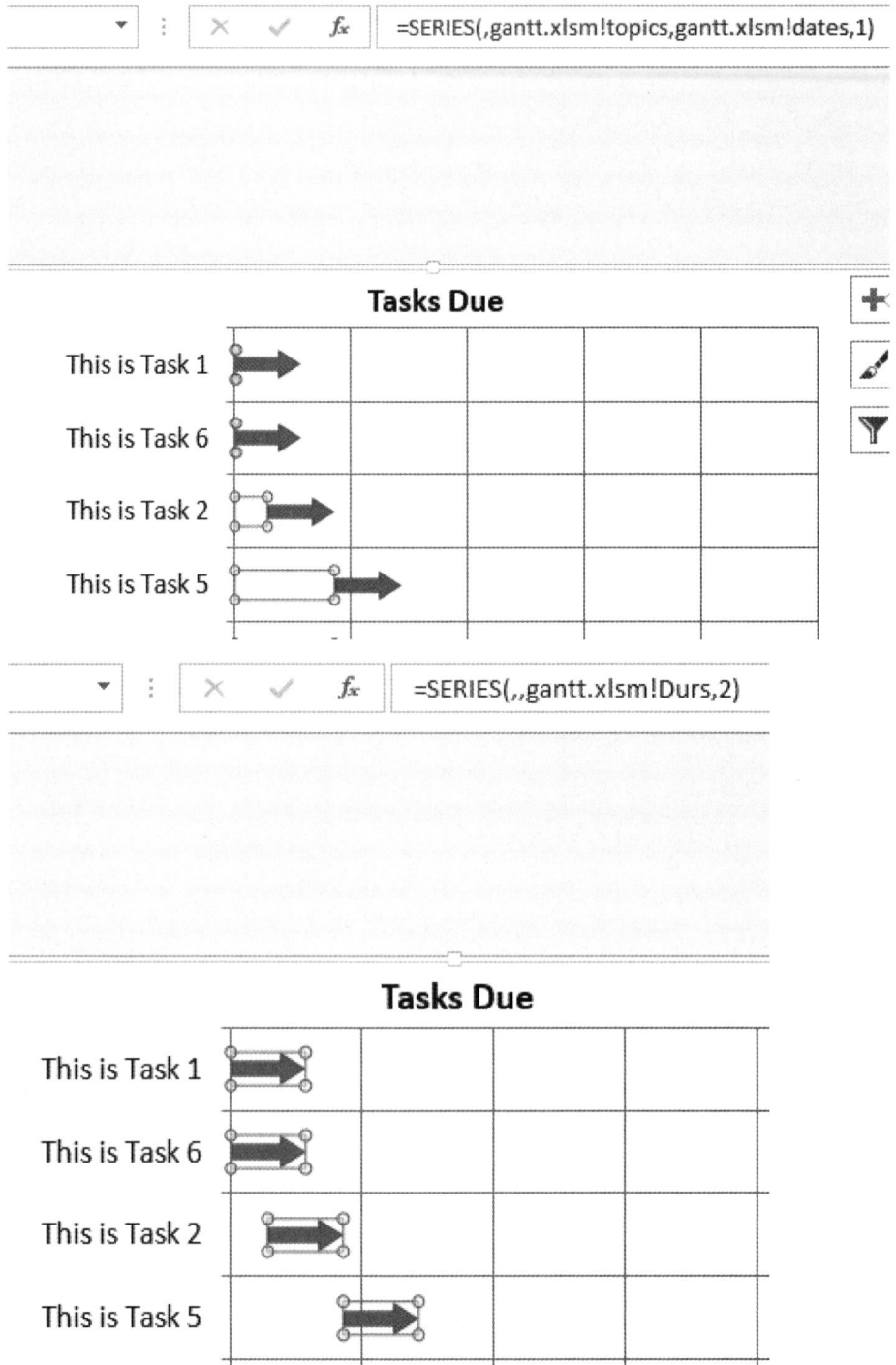

The first is a series that was formatted to not show, and the SERIES formula has topics and dates as its X and Y values. The second SERIES formula has only Durs as its Y values. These values are on the hidden sheet. Here's a look at this involved but useful sheet:

	A	B	C [	E	F	G	H I	J	K	L	M	N
1							8					4
2	This is Task 1	10/8/2011	2	2	This is Task 1	10/8/2011		1.02		This is Task 1	10/4/2011	4
3	This is Task 2	10/10/2011	3	3	This is Task 2	10/10/2011		3.03		This is Task 6	10/4/2011	4
4	This is Task 3	10/23/2011	4	4	This is Task 3	10/23/2011		6.04		This is Task 2	10/6/2011	4
5	0	1/0/1900		49	This is Task 5	10/14/2011		4.05		This is Task 5	10/10/2011	4
6	0	1/0/1900		50	This is Task 6	10/8/2011		1.06		This is Task 8	10/10/2011	4
7	0	1/0/1900		96	This is Task 7	11/1/2011		8.07		This is Task 3	10/19/2011	4
8	0	1/0/1900		97	This is Task 8	10/14/2011		4.08		This is Task 9	10/21/2011	4
9	0	1/0/1900		98	This is Task 9	10/25/2011		7.09		This is Task 7	10/28/2011	4
10	0	1/0/1900		#NUM!	#NUM!	#NUM!		#NUM!		#NUM!	#NUM!	4
11	0	1/0/1900		#NUM!	#NUM!	#NUM!		#NUM!		#NUM!	#NUM!	4

The range named topics is in L2:L9, dates is in M2:M9, and Durs is in N2:N9, so all the data for the chart is in L2:N9. If you add four tasks to any of the three sheets, the range ends up being L2:N13. That is, it automatically expands or contracts. One other key named range here is Cht, which is used to make these other ranges and is in G2:G9; it also self-adjusts, depending on the charts. All the #NUM! errors shown are not mistakes but are used later, as you will see.

Here's the formula for cell A2:

A2	▼	:	×	✓	fx	=INDIRECT("Info1!B"&ROW(A2))

	A	B	C [	E	F	G	H
1							8
2	This is Task 1	10/8/2011	2	2	This is Task 1	10/8/2011	
3	This is Task 2	10/10/2011	3	3	This is Task 2	10/10/2011	
4	This is Task 3	10/23/2011	4	4	This is Task 3	10/23/2011	
5		0	1/0/1900		49	This is Task 5	10/14/2011

This is filled down to row 48 (encompassing 47 rows of tasks for the Info1 sheet), but you could easily use more or fewer rows:

A48	▼	:	×	✓	fx	=INDIRECT("Info1!B"&ROW(A48))

	A	B	C [	E	F	G	H I
46	0	1/0/1900	#NUM!	#NUM!	#NUM!		
47	0	1/0/1900	#NUM!	#NUM!	#NUM!		
48	0	1/0/1900	#NUM!	#NUM!	#NUM!		
49	This is Task 5	10/14/2011	49	#NUM!	#NUM!	#NUM!	
50	This is Task 6	10/8/2011	50	#NUM!	#NUM!	#NUM!	
51		0	1/0/1900	#NUM!	#NUM!	#NUM!	

If you start with the formula =INDIRECT("Info1!B2") in cell A2, you can't fill this down because the formula will always point to B2 since it's inside the quotes. If you use INDIRECT, when someone inserts, deletes, or adds data, this will still work instead of possibly creating #REF! errors.

Starting in A49, there's a similar formula for the Info2 tab: =INDIRECT("'In-fo2'!B"&ROW(A2)). This formula is also filled down 47 rows, to A95, and then A96:A142 has the same formula except for Info3 instead of Info2.

Column B has exactly the same formula, but instead or referencing column B, it references column C of each sheet:

B2	▼	:	✕	✓	*fx*	=INDIRECT("Info1!C"&ROW(B2))

◢	A	B	C [	E	F	G	H I
1							8
2	This is Task 1	10/8/2011	2	2	This is Task 1	10/8/2011	
3	This is Task 2	10/10/2011	3	3	This is Task 2	10/10/2011	
4	This is Task 3	10/23/2011	4	4	This is Task 3	10/23/2011	

The formula is filled down to C2:C142:

C2	▼	:	✕	✓	*fx*	=IF(A2=0,"",ROW(A2))

◢	A	B	C [	E	F	G
1						
2	This is Task 1	10/8/2011	2	2	This is Task 1	10/8/2
3	This is Task 2	10/10/2011	3	3	This is Task 2	10/10/2
4	This is Task 3	10/23/2011	4	4	This is Task 3	10/23/2
5	0	1/0/1900		49	This is Task 5	10/14/2
6	0	1/0/1900		50	This is Task 6	10/8/2
49	This is Task 5	10/14/2011	49	#NUM!	#NUM!	#NUM
50	This is Task 6	10/8/2011	50	#NUM!	#NUM!	#NUM
51	0	1/0/1900		#NUM!	#NUM!	#NUM

The screen is split here so you can see the numbers in rows 49:50 as well. (Note that there are also numbers in C96:C98.)

E2 contains the formula =SMALL($C$2:$C$142,ROW(A1))

	A	B	C [	E	F	G	H
1							8
2	This is Task 1	10/8/2011	2	2	This is Task 1	10/8/2011	
3	This is Task 2	10/10/2011	3	3	This is Task 2	10/10/2011	
4	This is Task 3	10/23/2011	4	4	This is Task 3	10/23/2011	
5	0	1/0/1900		49	This is Task 5	10/14/2011	
6	0	1/0/1900		50	This is Task 6	10/8/2011	
7	0	1/0/1900		96	This is Task 7	11/1/2011	
8	0	1/0/1900		97	This is Task 8	10/14/2011	
9	0	1/0/1900		98	This is Task 9	10/25/2011	
10	0	1/0/1900		#NUM!	#NUM!	#NUM!	

You can now see all the rows containing data, contiguous-
ly. In this case, the formula fills E2:E9 with numbers. The formula is =SMALL($C$2:$C$142,ROW(A1)), which in row 2 is
=SMALL($C$2:$C$142,1), in row 3 is =SMALL($C$2:$C$142,2), etc.

F2 contains this simple formula:

```
=INDEX(A:A,E2)
```

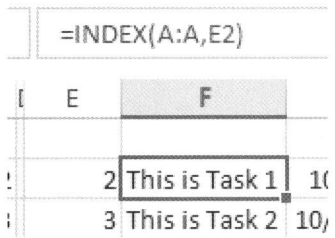

[	E	F	
!	2	This is Task 1	1(
;	3	This is Task 2	10/

When all the tasks are put together, G2 contains:

```
=INDEX(B:B,E2)
```

E	F	G	H	I
			8	
2	This is Task 1	10/8/2011		
3	This is Task 2	10/10/2011		
4	This is Task 3	10/23/2011		

Now all the dates are put together. There are just two problems left:

- The dates are not in sequence, so a bar chart would show this in the
  wrong sequence. (A Gantt chart is a type of bar chart.)

- How do we know which range to use once the dates *are* in the right
  sequence; the chart grows/shrinks, and it needs to reference the correct
  number of rows.

To find out how many rows are needed, you can use cell H1:

```
{=MATCH(TRUE,ISERROR(G:G),0)-2}
```

E	F	G	H	I	J
			8		
2	This is Task 1	10/8/2011			1
3	This is Task 2	10/10/2011			3
4	This is Task 3	10/23/2011			6
49	This is Task 5	10/14/2011			4
50	This is Task 6	10/8/2011			1
96	This is Task 7	11/1/2011			8
97	This is Task 8	10/14/2011			4
98	This is Task 9	10/25/2011			7
#NUM!	#NUM!	#NUM!			#NU
#NUM!	#NUM!	#NUM!			#NU
#NUM!	#NUM!	#NUM!			#NU

Note that this is an array formula because of ISERROR(G:G), so you enter it by using Ctrl+Shift+Enter (using just Enter would create #VALUE!). It's the only array formula in this example.

The formula searches for the error (#NUM!) in column G. In this example, it's in G10, but there are eight entries (G2:G9), so 2 is subtracted from the result. (The dates of interest here start in row 2, and you don't want to include the #NUM! error; that's why 2 is subtracted.) Cht is defined as =OFFSET($G$2,0,0,$H$1,1), which is =OFFSET(G$2,0,0,8,1), which is G2:G9. (Of course, the tab name is appended, and the actual formula in the definition is =OFFSET(Data!$G$2,0,0,-Data!$H$1,1), but Data! has been removed here for ease of explanation.)

To "sequence" the dates with formulas instead of actually sorting, you can assign them numbers with the RANK formula, but in case of ties, you can add a fraction to the result, namely the ROW()/100:

```
=RANK(G2,Cht,1)+ROW()/100
```

E	F	G	H	I	J	K
			8			
2	This is Task 1	10/8/2011			1.02	This
3	This is Task 2	10/10/2011			3.03	This
4	This is Task 3	10/23/2011			6.04	This
49	This is Task 5	10/14/2011			4.05	This

Notice that 10/8/2011 is really a rank of 1, but 2/100 is added, giving 1.02, so the second 10/8/2011, five rows down, would also be 1, but now it's 1.06. You'll see shortly why this is important.

Also notice that 10/14/2011 is in there twice, assigned 4.05 and 4.08.

It's time to finally get to one of the values used in the chart—the first task:

```
=INDEX(OFFSET(Cht,,-1),MATCH(SMALL(OFFSET(Cht,,3),ROW(A1)),OFFSET(Ch
```

E	F	G	H	I	J	K	L	M	N
			8						4
2	This is Task 1	10/8/2011			1.02		This is Task 1	10/4/2011	4

The first task is the one with the earliest date. Task 1 has a date of 10/4/2011, as does Task 6. Let's examine the formula shown in the formula bar for L2.

When this selection is evaluated (by pressing F9):

```
=INDEX(OFFSET(Cht,,-1),MATCH(SMALL(OFFSET(Cht,,3),ROW(A1)),OFFSET(Cht,,3),0))
```

we see:

```
=INDEX(OFFSET(Cht,,-1),MATCH({1.02},OFFSET(Cht,,3),0))
```

OFFSET(Cht,,3) is three columns to the right of Cht, which is J2:J9. It matches the smallest number in J2:J9 (which is 1.02) to the same set of numbers. This gives:

```
=INDEX(OFFSET(Cht,,-1),MATCH({1.02},{1.02;3.03;6.04;4.05;1.06;8.07;4.08;7.09},0))
```

or:

```
=INDEX(OFFSET(Cht,,-1),{1})
```

or:

```
This is Task 1
```

OFFSET(Cht,,-1) is the column to the left of Cht, or F2:F9.

Repeating this for L3, we see this sequence:

```
=INDEX(OFFSET(Cht,,-1),MATCH(SMALL(OFFSET(Cht,,3),ROW(A2)),OFFSET(Cht,,3),0))
```

G	H	I	J	K	L	M	N	O	P	Q
	8						4			
1	10/8/2011		1.02		This is Task 1	10/4/2011	4			
2	10/10/2011		3.03		This is Task 6	10/4/2011	4			

=INDEX(OFFSET(Cht,,-1),MATCH(SMALL(OFFSET(Cht,,3),ROW(A2)),OFFSET(Cht,,3),0))

or:

=INDEX(OFFSET(Cht,,-1),MATCH({1.06},OFFSET(Cht,,3),0))

then:

=INDEX(OFFSET(Cht,,-1),MATCH({1.06},OFFSET(Cht,,3),0))

or:

=INDEX(OFFSET(Cht,,-1),MATCH({1.06},{1.02;3.03;6.04;4.05;1.06;8.07;4.08;7.09},0))

then:

=INDEX(OFFSET(Cht,,-1),MATCH({1.06},{1.02;3.03;6.04;4.05;1.06;8.07;4.08;7.09},0))

or:

=INDEX(OFFSET(Cht,,-1),{5})

or This is Task 6.

Similarly, to get the dates, we use:

=INDEX(Cht,MATCH(SMALL(OFFSET(Cht,,3),ROW(B1)),OFFSET(Cht,,3),0))-$N$1

	G	H	I	J	K	L	M	N	O	P
		8						4		
1	10/8/2011			1.02		This is Task 1	10/4/2011	4		

Where did 10/4/2011 come from? The earliest date was 10/8/2011. Notice that the end of the formula has -$N$1, (which has a plain 4 in it). The rest of column N has =$N$1. Subtracting four days from all the dates enables you to use all the 4s as the length of the line (arrow), so in the chart, the arrow points to the end date of its task.

Now for three more definitions:

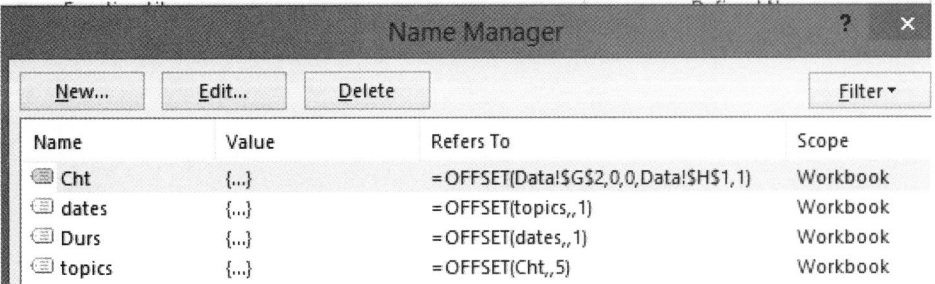

topics is defined as five columns to the right of Cht. If you use this strategy, you don't need the more complicated formula that Cht uses, namely OFFSET with cell H1.

dates is defined as one column to the right of topics, and Durs is defined as one column to the right of dates. So they're all offset from Cht.

That's basically it! To see the difference in the chart if you change, say, N1 to 7, all that's different is that the arrows are longer:

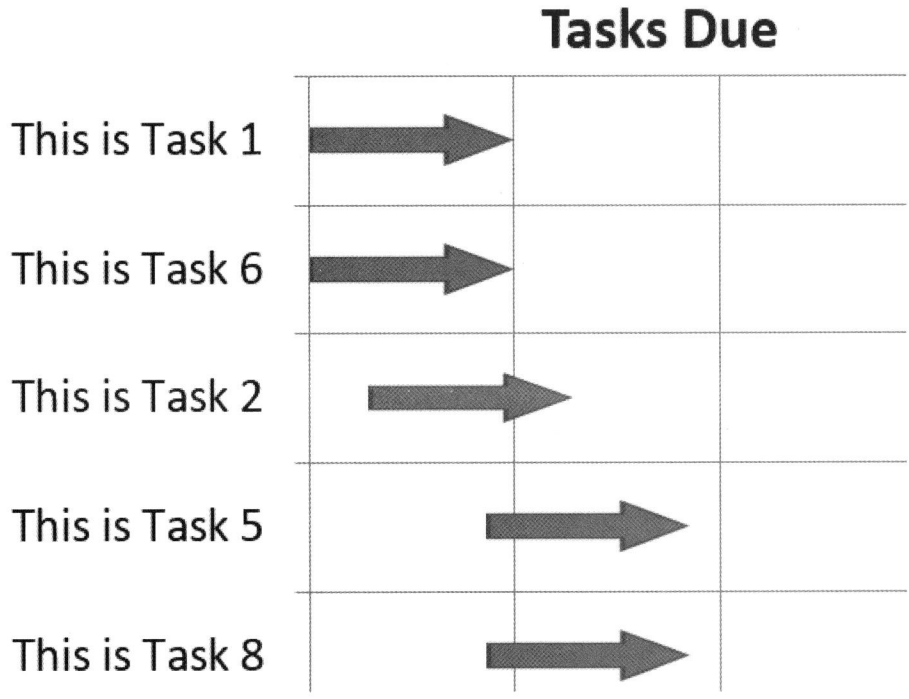

But how do you get the arrows? The original chart looked like this:

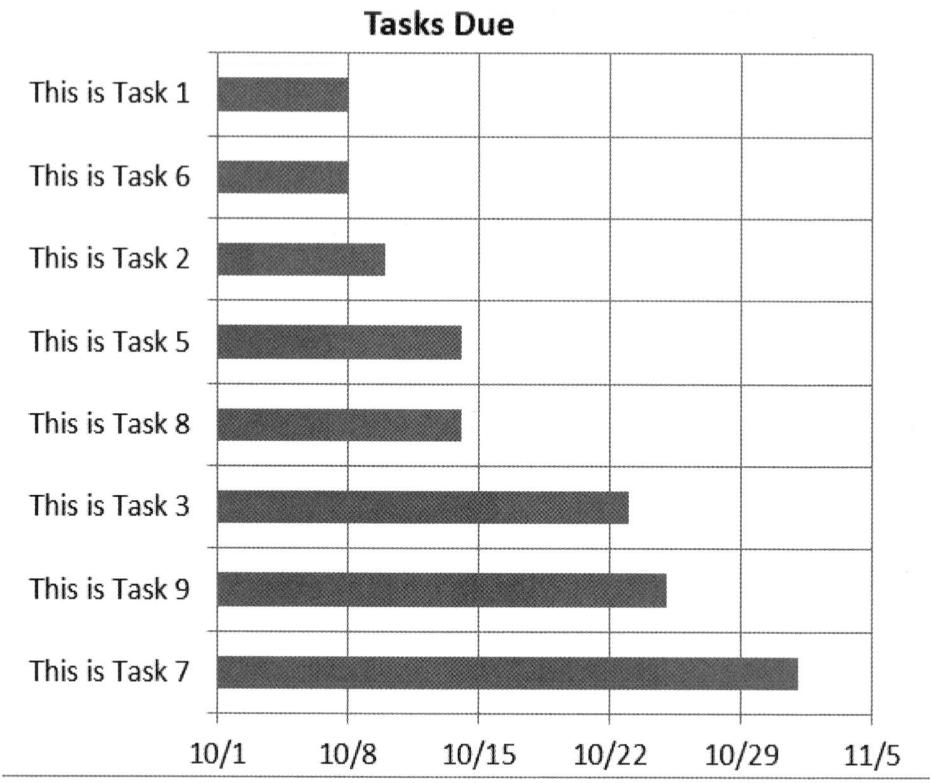

Tasks Due
This is Task 1
This is Task 6
This is Task 2
This is Task 5
This is Task 8
This is Task 3
This is Task 9
This is Task 7
10/1
10/8
10/15
10/22
10/29
11/5

To get the arrows, you select the first series and make it invisible:

Tasks Due
This is Task 1
This is Task 6
This is Task 2
This is Task 5
This is Task 8
This is Task 3
This is Task 9
This is Task 7
10/1
10/8
10/15
10/22
10/29
11/5
Format Data Series
SERIES OPTIONS
FILL
No fill
Solid fill
Gradient fill
Picture or texture fill
Pattern fill
Automatic
Invert if negative
BORDER

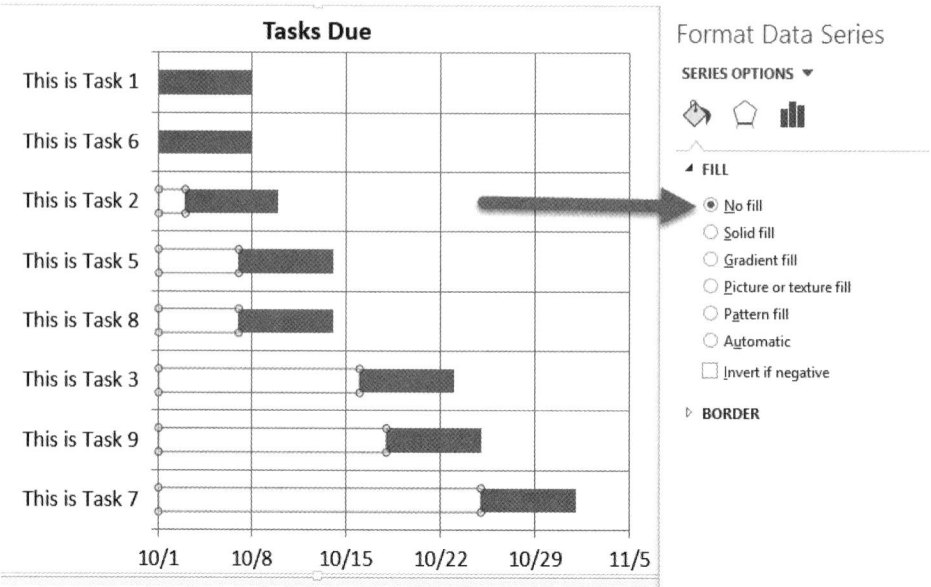

Then you draw an arrow via Insert/Shapes/Block Arrows:

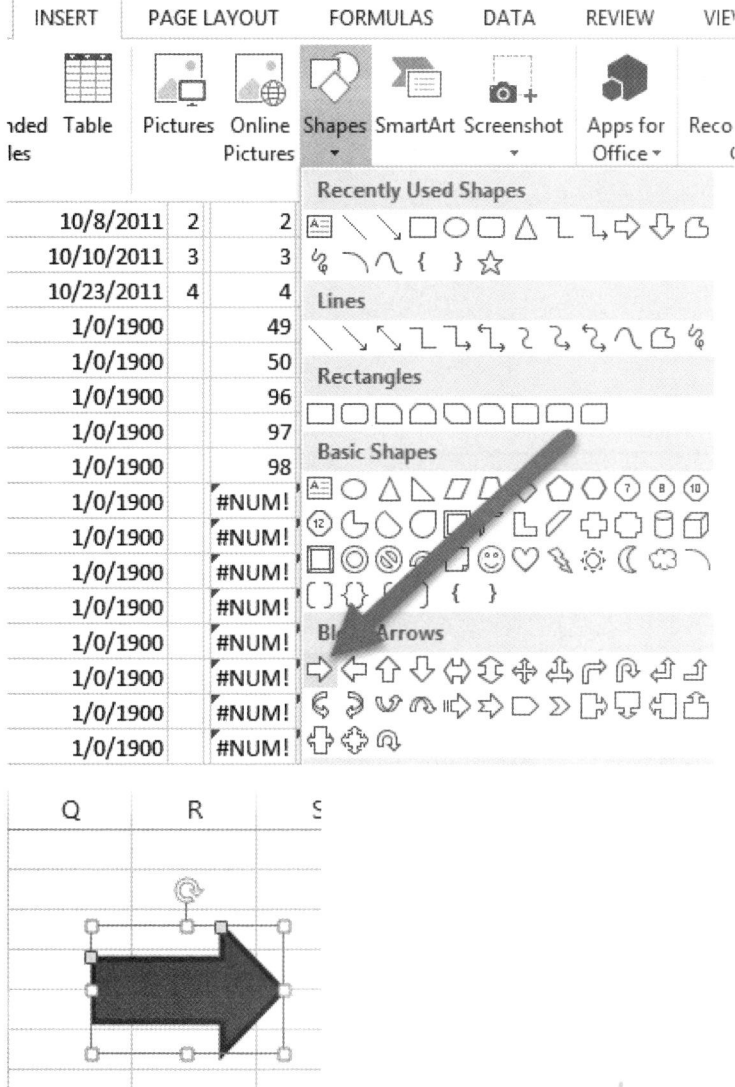

Then you select the arrow and copy it, select the second series, and paste the arrow.

Oh, here's the little macro mentioned earlier (Right-click the sheet tab, select View Code, and enter this):

```
Private Sub Chart_Activate()
   Application.CalculateFullRebuild
   On Error Resume Next
   ActiveChart.Axes(xlValue).MinimumScale = _
      Sheets("Data").Range("M2").Value
End Sub
```

This runs when then sheet is activated and changes the scale on the Value axis to match the earliest date. Cell M2 contains this earliest date, as shown before:

=INDEX(Cht,MATCH(SMALL(OFFSET(Cht,,3),ROW(B1)),OFFSET(Cht,,3),0))-$N$1

G	H	I	J	K	L	M	N	O	P
	8						4		
10/8/2011			1.02		This is Task 1	10/4/2011	4		
10/10/2011			2 02		This is Task 6	10/4/2011	4		

Protecting Tables of Data

This figure shows a small table in AB1:AC9:

AB	AC
Year	Amount
2005	1,803
2006	2,335
2007	5,611
2008	5,065
2009	1,340
2010	6,230
2011	3,367
2012	8,921

Back in columns A:C, you have some other unrelated data:

	A	B	C
1	1/1/2015	data	data
2	1/2/2015	data	data
3	1/3/2015	data	data
4	1/4/2015	data	data
5	1/5/2015	data	data
6	1/7/2015	data	data
7	1/8/2015	data	data
8	1/9/2015	data	data
9	1/10/2015	data	data
10	1/11/2015	data	data
11	1/12/2015	data	data

You notice that the data for 1/6/2015 is missing, so you insert a row. You don't realize that when you do this, you're messing up the data in the table in AB:AC, partly because it's not in view—it's scrolled off the screen. How can you prevent this kind of thing from happening? You can protect the range from inadvertent row (or column) insertions. How? Just add a do-nothing array formula next to your table:

| | *fx* | {=0} |

AA	AB	AC
0	Year	Amount
0	2005	1,803
0	2006	2,335
0	2007	5,611
0	2008	5,065
0	2009	1,340
0	2010	6,230
0	2011	3,367
0	2012	8,921

In this case, you select AA1:AA9 and enter =0 as an array (using Ctrl+-Shift+Enter). Then, when you try to insert a row back in the left part of the work-sheet, you get this message:

	A	B	C	D	E	F	G
1	1/1/2015	data	data				
2	1/2/2015	data	data				
3	1/3/2015	data	data				
4	1/4/2015	data	data				
5	1/5/2015	data	data				
6	1/7/2015	data	data				
7	1/8/2015	data	data				
8	1/9/2015	data	data				
9	1/10/2015	data	data				
10	1/11/2015	data	data				
11	1/12/2015	data	data				
12							

Microsoft Excel ✕

⚠ You cannot change part of an array.

OK

This is usually an unwanted message, but in this case, it saves the day!

Did You Know…? (a potpourri of miscellaneous ideas)

Going to the Previous Cursor Position in VBA

Did you know that VBA enables you to go to the previous cursor position? For example, here's a short piece of code in which one of the statements references another routine. Without even running the code, you can right-click next to or inside the text AnotherRoutine and see where it's defined:

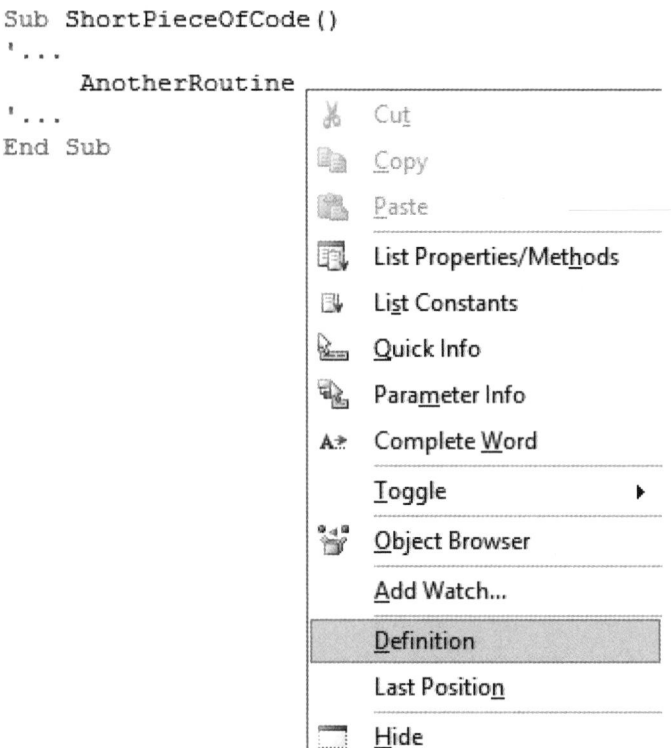

```
Sub ShortPieceOfCode()
'...
     AnotherRoutine
'...
End Sub
```

Here's the procedure (which is in a different module):

```
Sub AnotherRoutine()
'...
'...
'...
End Sub
```

Notice that the cursor is blinking in the line directly under Sub. How do you get back to where you were? Notice the Last Position command in the figure above, right under Definition. If you issue that command now:

Sub AnotherRoutine()

✂	Cut
📋	Copy
📋	Paste
🔃	List Properties/Methods
🔽	List Constants
🔖	Quick Info
🔧	Parameter Info
A⋗	Complete Word
	Toggle ▶
📦	Object Browser
	Add Watch...
	Definition
	Last Position

You wind up back in the place where you issued the Definition command. If the cursor has been in many places, you can issue Last Position repeatedly to trace the path of the various places you've visited.

Going Directly to a VBA Procedure

You can get to a VBA procedure directly, while not in the VBE, from Excel's Go To or Name box. For example, when you issue this command, Excel takes you directly to the code in the VBA:

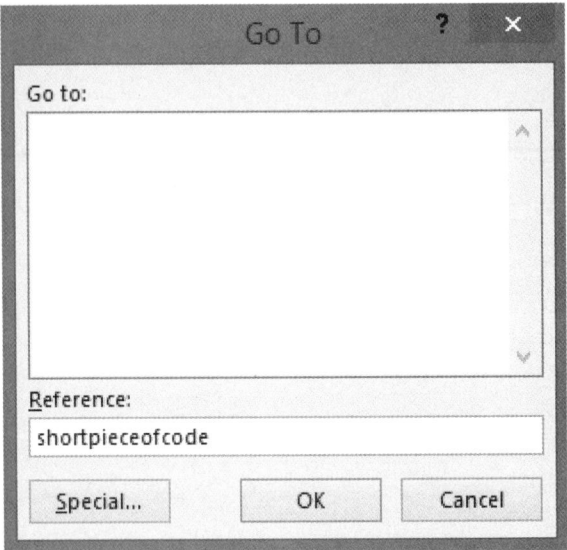

You can get the same effect by typing in the Name box:

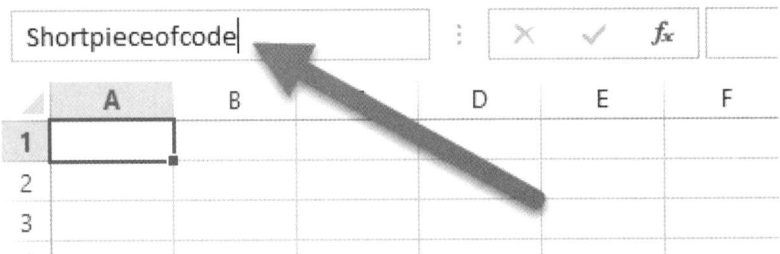

Of course, if you have a range name that is the same as a procedure name, the range name will be selected, not the procedure in VBA.

Entering Symbols

To get the © symbol, you simply type (c), and Excel automatically turns it into the ©. But if you want (c) and not the copyright symbol, as soon as Excel turns it into the symbol, just press Ctrl+Z. This is not just an Excel trick, by the way, but works in other Microsoft products as well.

Using Ctrl+Spacebar

When typing VBA code, you should take advantage of "complete word", or Ctrl/j. You can type something like Appl and then press Ctrl+Spacebar to have Excel automatically fill in the rest. For example, in the Immediate window, you can type App and press Ctrl+Spacebar to get this:

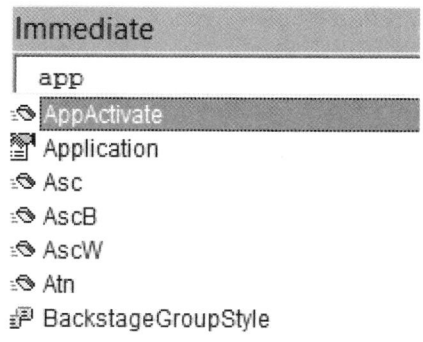

Excel supplies all the possibilities starting with App and alphabetically afterward.

You can also use this trick when you have a long variable defined to avoid typing the whole variable name. For example, if you have a long name such as ThisIsADatabasePointer defined, when you type thi and press Ctrl+Spacebar, Excel supplies the possibilities shown here:

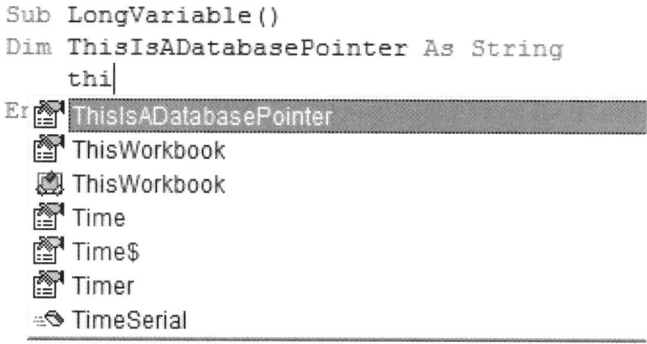

You can then select the one you want and press Tab to insert it into your code.

Replacing some cells' contents

Say that you have a formula like this:

=IF(Amount>=30,IF(Amount>=45,Amount*0.5,Amount*0.2),Amount*0.16)

Suppose that you want to change Amount to Amt in this formula, but you don't want the word Amount in cells A3 and A5 in this figure below to change:

A2	▼	:	✕	✓	fx	=IF(Amount>=30,IF(Amount>=45,Amount*0.5,Amount*0.2),Amount*0.16) and you
	A	B	C	D	E	F	G	H	I	J	K	L
1	Suppose you have a long formula which has text which repeats several times such as:
2	=IF(Amount>=30,IF(Amount>=45,Amount*0.5,Amount*0.2),Amount*0.16) and you
3	decide that In THIS formula, you want "Amount" to read "Amt", but not throughout the
4	worksheet. To change it, one thing you could do is edit each one in the formula bar
5	because using Find & Select/Replace would change ALL occurrences of Amount to Amt. Or
6	would it? Find & Select/Replace works on all cells if there's only one cell selected.
7	Otherwise, it works on the current selection. So, you only need to select this cell twice.
8	To do that, select it once, then hold the <ctrl> key and select it again! Now, the Replace
9	works just fine!

Excel limits your changes to the selected cells (or the whole worksheet, if one cell is selected), but you can override this by selecting the cell twice. In this case, by clicking cell A2 and Ctrl+clicking it again, you limit your changes to that one cell.

Searching Backward Through a Worksheet

If you want to search backward through a worksheet, all you need to do is hold down the Shift key while clicking Find in the dialog. This works with the wild-cards * and ? as well.

Index

About the Author, Bob Umlas

Bob is the longest-running Excel MVP. Here are some observations about Bob by his fellow MVP's:

"A veteran Most Valuable Profession (MVP) in Excel, Bob is part of the MVP furniture, so much so that I think I accidentally sat on him once (sorry Bob!). He has always been keen on his Excel quizzes and none was ever better answered than, "Who's that?" when his cheerful mugshot was adorning half the flagpoles at Chez Microsoft for one MVP Summit, as the Excel Powers That Be recognised his unwavering gift for finding every last bug. With a grin like the Cheshire Cat himself, it was a moment to be proud of. He must have hesitated for a second or two before reeling off five more helpful tips before you could press "r97c12:r97c24" and run Flight Simulator in Excel!" - Liam Bastick, SumProduct.com

"Bob Umlas is a master of Excel, and all its strange quirks and hidden magic tricks. He loves to share his knowledge, and Bob's enthusiasm for our favorite spreadsheet program is inspiring. If Bob doesn't know how to do something in Excel, it probably can't be done!" - Debra Dalgleish, Contextures.com

"Bob Umlas loves exploiting Excel bugs and turning them into tricks. So I showed Bob my rollover technique, which I thought he would appreciate. He then showed Microsoft Excel program manager David Gainer the rollover trick. When Dave saw it he said, "oh, we need to get rid of that!" Bob Umlas later told me this at guest reception dinner and I yelled, "Noooooooo!"; the rollover technique was probably the only original thing I've contributed to the Excel community. It's been two years since that then and, like Bob, the rollover technique hasn't gone anywhere." - Jordan Goldmeier, Cambia Factor

"Bob, not only an Excel magician, but let him loose with a pack of cards and he will amaze you!" - Roger Govier

"I was in NYC as a judge for the world financial modelling championships. Bob was a guest in the audience. As 16 of the brightest competitors tried to solve an Excel formula in the fewest characters, I could see Bob out of the corner of my eye trying something on my laptop. In 75% of the cases, Bob quickly beat the best solution from the contestants." - Bill Jelen, MrExcel.com

"I remember the first time I met him at an MVP summit. He walked up up in a shirt that said 'Ask me about my vow of silence' and proceeded to ask me if I knew how to do something or other with Excel. I said 'Wait... Tell me about your vow of silence?' 'I didn't take one. Now do you know how to do that in Excel?'" - Ken Puls, ExcelGuru.ca

"One bit of info I noticed about Bob was this past Summit, when he is a ringer at the table tennis (ping pong) table. I did not get to play him because the session breaks were too short and I used to play a lot when I was younger. But he was smoking the dudes he was playing against that week and he probably would have whupped me too." - Tom Urtis, Atlas Programming Management